FOOD LOVERS'
GUIDE TO
PHOENIX
& SCOTTSDALE

Help Us Keep This Guide Up to Date

We would love to hear from you concerning your experiences with this guide and how you feel it could be improved and kept up to date. Please send your comments and suggestions to:

editorial@GlobePequot.com

Thanks for your input, and happy travels!

FOOD LOVERS' SERIES

FOOD LOVERS'
GUIDE TO
PHOENIX
& SCOTTSDALE

The Best Restaurants, Markets & Local Culinary Offerings

1st Edition

Katarina Kovacevic

gpp

Guilford, Connecticut

Editor: Kevin Sirois
Project Editor: Lynn Zelem
Layout Artist: Mary Ballachino
Text Design: Sheryl Kober
Illustrations © Jill Butler with additional art by Carleen Moira Powell and MaryAnn Dubé
Maps: Sue Murray © Morris Book Publishing, LLC

ISBN 978-0-7627-7314-5

Printed in the United States of America
10 9 8 7 6 5 4 3 2 1

All the information in this guidebook is subject to change. We recommend that you call ahead to obtain current information before traveling.

Contents

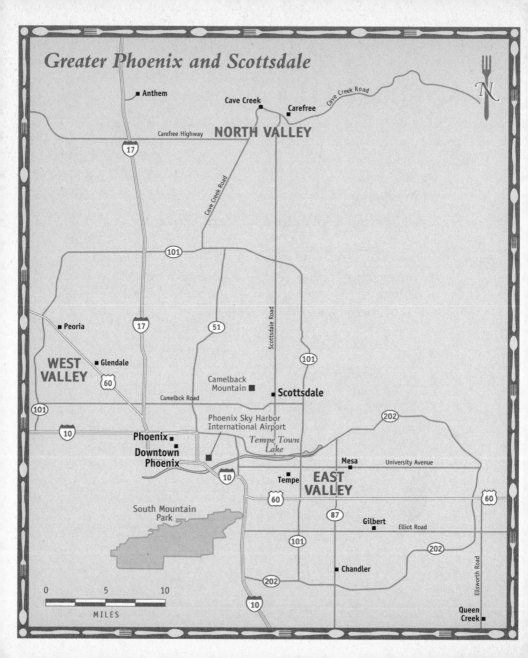

Recipes, 231

About the Author

Katarina Kovacevic was once on the other side of the spectrum as a public relations representative for the local tourism industry and later as an agency account executive handling several restaurant and hospitality accounts. But, they say, a girl never forgets her first love. For Katarina, that's writing. Her work as a full-time freelance writer has been published in national and international magazines like *Sunset* and *USA Today,* locally in *The Arizona Republic* and *Arizona Foothills,* and online at SheKnows.com and AOL Travel. She lives in Gilbert, Arizona, with her boyfriend, Stjepan, where she is still stumbling upon new culinary gems after three years.

Acknowledgments

Cheers to the people who made this book possible: All of my foodie friends who take on a new restaurant like I imagine sailors would a maiden voyage—with excitement and a tiny bit of craziness; the Greater Phoenix area's food bloggers, whose posts, tweets, and Facebook statuses oftentimes turned me on to a new restaurant weeks before any print reviews were published; and a kick-butt assistant, Michelle Lauer, for putting her enviable organizational and wordsmith skills to work on the massive appendices and Home Grown Chains and Food Trucks sidebars of this book.

And there's no way I could wrap this project up without mentioning my big brother, Josip, for checking in on the project every day and providing words of encouragement when I was two words away from going postal; my parents for being proud of me, no matter what I do; and my boyfriend, Stjepan, for listening to all of my madness and accompanying me to the local coffee shop for weekend work sessions, even when he didn't have anything to work on himself.

And to my editor Kevin Sirois, who made my first step into the world of book writing (almost) a breeze with his hilarious e-mails and stay-calm personality. Thank you!

Introduction

Phoenix & Scottsdale: Unchained & Evolved

Dining out in Phoenix and Scottsdale once meant you had to choose between the lesser of two evils: chain restaurants with their bland food and unimaginative menus, or hokey establishments where the steak was as tough as the leather on your server's cowboy boots. True, there are some now-iconic places that have been slinging gourmet goods for years, but, until somewhat recently, these spots were few and far between. Then, in the early 2000s, a boom in the housing industry prompted a massive influx of migrants from across the country, catapulting Greater Phoenix into the position of the sixth largest city in the United States. A city that always had the makings of a world-class metropolis—nearly perfect weather, five-star resorts, a captivating Sonoran Desert setting—was thrust into the spotlight and residents as a whole began developing a more sophisticated palate. Suddenly, Phoenix and Scottsdale were major contenders in the national culinary world.

But even in the midst of this gastronomic evolution, Phoenix and Scottsdale have managed to preserve the very real, very proud

Old West attitude that is what makes the region such an alluring place. You can still order rattlesnake, T-bone steak, and some of the best classic hamburgers you'll 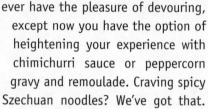 ever have the pleasure of devouring, except now you have the option of heightening your experience with chimichurri sauce or peppercorn gravy and remoulade. Craving spicy Szechuan noodles? We've got that. Dying for a slice of European-style pizza? We have it, too. Want to get your hands on some sweetbreads ragout? No problem. It's all here.

It's probably this same bold, autonomous Western spirit that spurred an uprising of independent, chef-owned restaurants that went to war with corporate big names who didn't have the meat and potatoes to back up their big talk. And, I'm happy to say, the good guys didn't just win the battle; they swept the whole freaking crusade. Phoenicians love to support local in every sense of the word. Outdoor markets with produce from area farms, mom-and-pop eateries, and food trucks aplenty; it's all on the menu. And while all of the recognition Phoenix and Scottsdale have received in recent years has caught the eye of several celebrity chefs who have sunk their chops into the area and opened their well-known boutique brands, the real stars of the show are the homegrown Arizona celebrity chefs who are on the front lines every day, working to preserve this hard-won reputation as one of the best dining destinations in the country.

This book is separated into different regions of Greater Phoenix and Scottsdale, and within each you'll find these features:

Neighborhood Map

Greater Phoenix and Scottsdale are broken up into geographical regions known simply as the North, West, and East Valleys, which are all basically groups of cities and towns. Because Downtown, Phoenix proper, and Scottsdale have enough dining options to constitute their own books entirely, we've called each out in its own special section. All of the spots included in this guidebook have been marked on the neighborhood maps.

Foodie Faves

This section is broad and includes any restaurant we think is worth a visit, from long-standing favorites to the latest on the scene.

Landmarks

The restaurants in this category have been around long before the population boom in the 2000s, and deserve much recognition for helping put Greater Phoenix and Scottsdale on the food map.

Farm-to-Table

The word "desert" brings to mind images of barren land and fruitless soil, but Greater Phoenix and Scottsdale's histories are actually rooted in agriculture. We tell you where to get the freshest bites in town.

Specialty Stores, Markets & Producers

Helping you navigate the long list of artisan bakeries, local butcher shops, and well-stocked farmers' markets, we give you a list of must-visit specialty stores.

Learn to Cook

Greater Phoenix and Scottsdale are home to a respected group of nationally acclaimed chefs and we explain how, and where, you can hone your skills.

Home Grown Chains Sidebars

Even if you don't live in Arizona, you've probably heard of these establishments at some point. These home grown restaurants evolved into statewide, regional, or national chains.

All-Star & Celebrity Chefs Sidebars

Greater Phoenix and Scottsdale have their fair share of acclaimed chefs, whether they're locally acclaimed culinary masters or nationwide TV personalities.

Recipes

At the back of this book, we give new meaning to the phrase "continued education" and help you create some of our favorite local dishes at home.

Price Code

We also included price information for restaurants using the following scale system for a single entree:

$	**Less than $10**
$$	**$10 to $20**
$$$	**More than $20**

Getting Around

Getting to Phoenix and Scottsdale is easy thanks to Phoenix Sky Harbor International Airport, one of the top 10 busiest airports in the United States. US Airways, Continental, Delta, and United Airlines—all of the big names fly in and out of Sky Harbor, and so do many budget companies like JetBlue and Southwest.

Once you're in the city, transportation options depend on your plans. If you're hoping for the grand tour and are scheduling meals that span multiple regions, renting a car is the most convenient way to go. And, thanks to a mostly north to south and east to west main street grid, navigating Greater Phoenix and Scottsdale is extremely easy. Printing driving directions from www.mapquest.com or www.maps.google.com, or renting a GPS system from the car facility, is more than enough, but buying a map never hurts and will only help you understand the system better. There are some instances, especially with newer establishments or in the outlying areas of town, where technology just hasn't caught up with physical addresses.

While the Valley Metro Light Rail, which opened in December 2008, is quick and affordable, it is somewhat limited in terms of its reach. The system spans from the East Valley in Mesa through Tempe and into northwest Phoenix with some fantastic food stops along the way, but in many cases additional transportation to your actual destination is needed from the Light Rail stop. Staying in Downtown Phoenix but want to visit Liberty Market in the East Valley? You could take the Light Rail to the Sycamore station in Mesa (the final stop on the route), but you'll have to cab it to Gilbert's Heritage District. The West and North Valleys and Scottsdale are missing Light Rail access altogether, but Light Rail is still convenient if you plan to stay and/or play anywhere along the line. PHXRailFood.com is the best resource for restaurants along the line.

If you are feeling particularly adventurous and have (a lot of) time to kill, you could always try your hand at the Valley Metro bus system, though I wouldn't recommend it. While the cost for a one-way ride is reasonable, the bus system is ineffective if you are trying to hit multiple restaurants in a limited timeframe. That's why, if you want to supplement your Light Rail adventures with some off-the-line restaurants, a rental car or taxi is the best recommendation. While cabs are readily available in more populated areas like Downtown Phoenix and Scottsdale, Greater Phoenix isn't New York City so have contact information

for local companies on hand. AAA Yellow Cab (www.aaayellowaz
.com) and Discount Cab (www.discountcab.com) are among the
most popular.

Keeping Up With Food News

The area of Greater Phoenix and Scottsdale is home to more than
3 million people who are all hungry for the latest food trend. Even
in a down economy and stalled local real estate market, or in some
cases because of these factors, the local dining scene can change
faster than Kim Kardashian can fall in love. At times it can be
daunting trying to process the wave of restaurant openings and
closings, like a never-ending game of Monopoly. Thankfully, Greater
Phoenix and Scottsdale has a dedicated foodie following—some
professionally trained, others self-taught—who are much more "on
it" than I could ever be. It's true that my jam-packed food blogroll
and stack of print subscriptions have always been a personal obsession but, when researching this book, they became much more than
just a favorite pastime. They became my life source. I've included
Twitter handles when available. You can follow me @Little_K.

Arizona Food Tours (www.ArizonaFoodTours.com): Arizona Food
Tours' "A Taste of Old Town Scottsdale" is a walking food and his-
torical tour of The West's Most Western Town. For $42 per person,
you get samples at 5 of the area's top restaurants and specialty
stores like the Mission and Outrageous Olive Oils. In the end, you'll

have consumed enough food to be considered lunch and also have much more of an appreciation for what started as a frontier town. The tour goes on rain or shine so pay attention to the weather report and wear comfortable shoes.

The Arizona Republic (www.dining.azcentral.com): I always assumed that every major newspaper in the country would have a robust food and drink beat. Recent travels have revealed that I am either extremely naive or very spoiled. Thankfully, though, Arizona's largest daily newspaper understands that food isn't just a carnal necessity, it's a passion, hobby, and—for some of us—a way of life. That's why Wednesday has quickly become my favorite day thanks to the *Arizona Republic* "Food & Drink" insert where experts like Howard Seftel and Barbara Yost share their recent finds. For more immediate satisfaction, I admit to visiting AZCentral .com regularly, where reviews are sometimes posted a couple of days before print versions are published.

Blog.ScottsdaleCVB.com: Because this is the official travel blog of the Scottsdale Convention & Visitors Bureau, all dining coverage tends to focus more on current events rather than actual reviews. One of the things I find most appealing about this blog is how easy it is to navigate, especially since they cover much more than just the restaurant scene. Even the dining section is broken down further into categories like chefs, cooking classes and events, resort dining, and exclusive dinners. Twitter: @scottsdaleaz.

DesertLivingToday.com: A true sign of the times, *Desert Living* was once a top luxury magazine in Greater Phoenix and Scottsdale that has since been replaced with an online version. Thankfully, all this has meant is that the DesertLivingToday.com crew is able to provide much more up-to-the-minute coverage, especially when it comes to the local dining scene. Their regular "Chow Down: This Week in Food Blogs" posts aren't just a good news resource, but they're also hilarious. Twitter: @DesertLivToday.

EATERAZ.com: While the name might hint otherwise, EATERAZ.com has no relation to the larger Eater.com family of websites. One part news, two parts satire, EATERAZ.com is a self-proclaimed "food gossip" site whose owners get a kick out of airing the local restaurant industry's dirty laundry. Many times, the hearsay they print ends up being true. Other times, they post corrected updates when announcements become "official news." But, at all times, they are funny, on the ball, and a worthwhile resource for the latest dining updates. Twitter: @eateraz.

EricEatsOut.com: I couldn't tell you what Eric looks like, or even his last name, but I can tell you that his blog always does one of two things: makes me hungry or makes me wish I was his best friend, if only to ride the coattails of his food-fueled blogging race without having to do any research myself. I like Eric's food blog because he doesn't take himself too seriously (as you've probably noted given the name of his blog), but his descriptions are always well written and the large photos are an added bonus. Rarely do I get through a post without drooling. (Sorry, too much information, I'm sure.) Twitter: @ericeatsout.

FoodiesLikeUs.com: Owner J. E. Pizarro and his stable of food bloggers cater to those of us (ahem) who center their social calendars on food. The Scottsdale-based company not only produces a regular e-newsletter with drool-worthy photos and reviews, but also throws some of the best food-focused parties in town. From cooking classes to private tastings and even a Light Rail Dine-Around, FoodiesLikeUs.com has done it all, and done it well. I've been to several of their events and only once have I ever seen a shortage of tastings, which was at a sushi restaurant. And, really, can anyone actually ever get full from sushi? Twitter: @foodieslikeus.

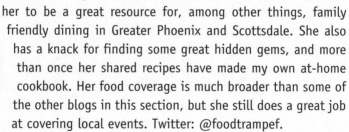

FoodTrampDiaries.com: The daughter of a German butcher, Erin from FoodTrampDiaries.com is herself a mom of two so I find her to be a great resource for, among other things, family friendly dining in Greater Phoenix and Scottsdale. She also has a knack for finding some great hidden gems, and more than once her shared recipes have made my own at-home cookbook. Her food coverage is much broader than some of the other blogs in this section, but she still does a great job at covering local events. Twitter: @foodtrampef.

GirlMeetsFork.com: Susie Timm, the "girl" behind GirlMeetsFork .com, has an entire photo gallery dedicated to meat. She lives for barbecue festivals and gets excited about things like head cheese, spare ribs, and smokers (the meat kind, not tobacco). But besides being an advocate for the carnivore community, she's also a great go-to source for information on spontaneous food events that are born from sheer love of a particular item rather than a desire to make money. Case in point: a "Grilled Cheese Throw Down" that had me at the word "cheese." Twitter: @susietimm.

Juxtapalate.com: To be fair, I should tell you that Ty Largo of Juxtapalate.com is a local food publicist whose clients are regularly featured on his blog. But, his agency also just so happens to represent some of the best independent restaurants in town so his rave reviews are oftentimes warranted. I'm not afraid to say that his blog is a personal favorite because Largo's writing style is every bit as sassy and self-deprecating as his real-life personality. What is particularly great about Juxtapalate.com are the photos, videos, and amusing illustrations that add to the story. Twitter: @juxtapalate.

MicheleLaudig.com: Michele Laudig is a restaurant critic, food writer, and blogger who was once the brains behind Chow Bella and the *Phoenix New Times'* dining section. She's a legit food critic, so you won't ever see her face anywhere on her blog, but what you will find is an insider's perspective into some of the best—and most obscure—restaurants in Arizona and beyond. What's great about Michele is that, after all of these years, she is still absolutely in love with her job and the local restaurant scene. She's not jaded, and that's hard to come by in this industry. This "agent of secrets" is always fun to follow on social media. Twitter: @michelelaudig.

MouthbySouthwest.com: Jess Harter is a longtime restaurant critic who used to cover the East Valley specifically for one of the area's daily newspapers. Now, he's taken his expertise to the blogosphere, expanding his coverage Valley-wide. Though, to this day, no one covers the East Valley quite like him. And, being an E.V. resident myself, I regularly visit Harter's blog for the kind of in-depth, substantial breakdown of flavor and texture that only a trained critic can provide. He's also great at keeping readers informed of the latest dining discounts, which he filters from various "deals" websites into a single easy-to-read post. Twitter: @mxsw.

PenAndFork.com: Gwen Ashley Walters is a trained chef who graduated from the local Scottsdale Culinary Institute and worked in kitchens across Arizona, including at the Boulders Resort & Golden Door Spa. She's also the author of three cookbooks and a regular contributor to *Phoenix* magazine. On PenAndFork.com, Walters partners with a handful of other enthusiastic food writers and covers everything from restaurant grand openings to easy tips for the at-home chef. Recently, she opened my eyes to the chocolate chipper tool and my life hasn't been the same since. Twitter: @chefgwen.

***Phoenix* Magazine** (www.phoenixmag.com): The monthly publication covers dining in Greater Phoenix and Scottsdale on a regular basis, but its annual special editions like "Best Restaurants" (January), "Best Bars" (March), "Best Things to Eat" (May), and "Best New Restaurants" (October), make it a must-have when planning your culinary excursions.

Phoenix New Times (www.phoenixnewtimes.com): While journalism for the purposes of shock and awe isn't my bag, I do appreciate the time and resources that the *Phoenix New Times* dedicates to the local food scene. Their critic is undercover when visiting restaurants for research purposes, so you know that the reviews will be straightforward. The Chow Bella blog (http://blogs.phoenixnew times.com/bella) is an extension of its print coverage with more immediate updates and their "Happy Hour Report Card" section is hands down the best place to get details on establishments where Happy Hour food specials are as good as the cocktails.

PHXRailFood.com: PHXRailFood.com highlights the best places to eat along the Valley Metro Light Rail line that connects Phoenix, Tempe, and Mesa. It has reviews of more than 130 restaurants that are either directly along the route or within a half-mile walk of a light rail station. It makes navigating the wide world of Greater Phoenix dining much easier. Twitter: @PHXRailFood.

TheHotSheetBlog.com: Like Scottsdale, Greater Phoenix also has its own blog that's run by the Convention & Visitors Bureau.

I find it to be particularly useful for updates on developments in Downtown Phoenix where the restaurant roster, thanks to recent openings of places like CityScape, seems to change on a daily basis. Twitter: @visitphoenix.

TheWildLavender.com: Nikki Buchanan has been a food writer for more than 25 years, holding posts at various publications across Greater Phoenix and Scottsdale. She seems to have an on-again, off-again relationship with her food blog, but when she does post to TheWildLavender.com, it's food nerding-out in its truest form. No one describes the silkiness of corn tamale or floral accents of a really good Moscato quite like Buchanan, so if you are a die-hard food snob (loud and proud, right?), you'll love her insights. Twitter: @TheWildLavender.

Festivals & Events

January

CRAVE Arizona, Scottsdale; www.cravearizona.com. What started as a fall food fete with the name Eats3 has shifted into the winter culinary celebration known as CRAVE Arizona. Focusing solely on independent restaurants in the Scottsdale area, the upside to CRAVE is the direct access you have to Arizona-based chefs and restaurants. The downside is the ticket prices for some of the smaller, more intimate events like the sommelier-led private dinners or Elixirs at the Loft, a more elaborate cocktail hour. The Grand Tasting, which closes out the 4-day event, is extremely accessible and worth the trip with past special appearances from big names like "Top Chef" Stephanie Izard and celebrity restaurateur Michael Mina, who opened Bourbon Steak at the nearby Fairmont Scottsdale Princess.

March

Great Arizona Beer Festival, Tempe; www.azbeer.com/tempe. Held at Tempe Beach Park, the Great Arizona Beer Festival is a massive event that attracts somewhere in the ballpark of 50,000 people every year. And while the emphasis here is on sipping, not noshing, the Great Arizona Beer Festival has rightfully earned its spot in this book because of its attention to seasonal, specialty craft brews like Cowboy Coffee Porter from Big Sky Brewing Company in Montana and the Organic Imperial Brown from Bison Brewing. Local companies make a fair showing, too. Some of my favorites included the Old Frog Grog oatmeal stout from Tempe's own Dave's Electric Brew Pub and SanTan's pale ale. But, I must admit, the people-watching is just as good as the beer that's on tap. Though it probably goes without saying, you must be at least 21 years old to enter.

Arizona BBQ Festival, Scottsdale; www.azbbqfestival.com. Started by Affordable Food Festivals, LLC, a duo of ex-publishing professionals turned food bloggers, the Arizona BBQ Festival sets the Scottsdale Waterfront aflame every spring with more than 40 barbecue teams—from world champions to novices—who are competing for a coveted prize of $20,000 and, let's be honest, the adoration of event attendees. It's a Kansas City Barbecue Society–sanctioned event, so the grub here is real and real good. Even Arizona Senator John McCain stops by for a taste. And, so do approximately 9,000 other 'cue fanatics who munch on $2 samples of the competitive food while listening to live music, taking in cooking demonstrations by local chefs like James Porter and Beau MacMillan, and letting their "mini me's" loose in the Kid's Zone. But the real belle of the barbecue ball is Whiskey Row, a tent-covered section where whiskey-based cocktails flow and area bartenders show off their skills.

Devoured, Phoenix; www.devourphoenix.com. It's been called the Olympics of Arizona food events, and for good reason. Not only does Devoured attract some of the best independent restaurants from Phoenix every March, but it's probably the most critically acclaimed food event in all of Greater Phoenix and Scottsdale, loved especially by top local food reviewers like Howard Seftel from the

Arizona Republic. Hosted by Local First Arizona and the Phoenix Art Museum, Devoured is particularly fun because it features all elements of the meal, from cocktails to dessert. I was in sweet-treat heaven at the exclusive, but affordable at $10 per ticket, Dessert Social.

April

My Nana's Best Tasting Salsa Challenge, Tempe; www.salsa challenge.com. While other food events in Greater Phoenix and Scottsdale are all about showcasing restaurants and established chefs, My Nana's Best Tasting Salsa Challenge is all about the little guy. Here, individuals and families from across Arizona descend upon Tempe to share their personal takes on America's number one condiment. (Yes, that's right, salsa is more popular than ketchup.) I almost never made it away from a booth without chatting up the competitors, but that just made the homemade *pico de gallos* and *salsas verdes* even sweeter (er, spicier) because I came to find that many of the recipes were passed down through multiple generations.

Scottsdale Culinary Festival, Scottsdale; www.scottsdaleculinary festival.org. As the nation's longest-running celebration of its kind, the Scottsdale Culinary Festival has been attracting foodies and chefs for more than 30 years. At first glance, Scottsdale Culinary

Festival may seem like it's more about the glitz and glamour than the food, but don't let its extra shiny exterior fool you. Yes, there's the Eat, Drink, & Be Pretty Party where attendees fawn over stiletto pumps rather than grilled prawns, but at its core Scottsdale Culinary Festival is a food lover's dream, no doubt in part due to the annual Friends of James Beard Benefit Dinner. If you're lucky enough to score a ticket—they're pricey at $200 per person—you'll have front row seats to watch some of the best James Beard–recognized masters in action, like Pastry Chef Nicole Plue of Cyrus in California and Jason Wilson, executive chef of Crush in Seattle. Locals come out in droves mostly for the Great Arizona Picnic, an outdoor grand finale of food and drink.

Forks & Corks, Downtown Phoenix; www.forksandcorks.org. While I don't necessarily recommend traveling to Greater Phoenix and Scottsdale specifically for Forks & Corks, the event definitely is worth checking out if you happen to be visiting at the start of April and have $65 to spend on a ticket. In 2011, the festival moved to Downtown Phoenix's new CityScape development and, while crowded and hard to navigate in some parts thanks to narrow streets, gained more of a big city vibe. Forks & Corks attracts a decent showing of restaurants in the Valley, most of which come from top area resorts like Frank & Albert's at the Biltmore and T. Cook's from the Royal Palms Resort. It's a happy hour–timed event—5:30 to 8:30 p.m.—so you'll find most attendees dressed in business or business casual attire.

September

Arizona Restaurant Week, Greater Phoenix & Scottsdale; www
.arizonarestaurantweek.com. For locals, Arizona Restaurant Week
is like Christmas in September. Every year, the event attracts more
than 100 restaurants that put together special 3-course tasting
menus (some with wine, beer, or cocktail
pairings) for the price of $30 or $40 per
person. The list of participating restaurants
continues to evolve, with more one-of-a-
kind establishments like Cork in Chandler
and Coup des Tartes in Phoenix jumping
on board every year. Check www.arizona
restaurantweek.com in the summer, usually

by July, for complete information on participating restaurants and
make reservations early because spots fill up fast. In 2011, a spring
Arizona Restaurant Week was added to the line-up, held mid-May.

October

Arizona Taco Festival, Scottsdale; www.aztacofestival.com.
Brought to you by the same quirky duo that puts on the Arizona
BBQ Festival, this fall event shines a spotlight on what the
Southwest, particularly Arizona, is really known for—its unbeatable
Mexican food. And, with local legends like Los Sombreros, Ticoz,
and the Mission in the line-up, you'll want to come hungry. The
concept is similar to the barbecue festival's, with teams competing

for a grand prize for the best taco, but entertainment at this festival is a bit more, well, festive with Lucha Libre Wrestling and the Hot Chili Pepper Eating Contest. I loved the Arizona Taco Festival because tasting portions, $2, are generous with at least 1 to 2 ounces of protein per sample in the form of either smaller Mexican "street" tacos or bits of larger ones. If that's not enough to fill you up, there's also a market of vendors selling larger meals.

Food Trucks

The only thing better than easily accessible food-on-the-go is delicious, easily accessible food-on-the-go. A nice alternative to typical fast food, Phoenix food trucks offer affordable and tasty eats that range from vegan- and vegetarian-friendly to Mexican and Filipino cuisine. **Phoenix Street Food** (www.phxstreetfood.org) is so in love with local mobile food vendors that they've dedicated an entire website and blog to the movement. Check it out for information on the latest events and locations of the food trucks.

Beet StrEAT, (480) 331-2338; http://beetstreat.com. Beet StrEAT is an affordable and convenient way to purchase groceries without leaving the house. Beet StrEAT, a mobile kitchen and market, is a shopping cart–less alternative to Whole Foods, Trader Joe's, and other organic and health food stores and markets. It has unprocessed foods and a made-to-order menu that changes and grows depending on what's freshest in local farmers' fields. Beet StrEAT doesn't have a set schedule yet, and typically cruises the open road looking for hungry customers. Follow the truck on Twitter @beetstreattruk to find it or check out www.facebook.com/beetstrEAT.

Carte Blanche Gourmet Tacos, (480) 277-1102; http://carte blanchegourmet.com. If you're visiting Arizona and reading this book, blinking, or thinking about your restaurant itinerary, you're partaking in an activity besides eating Mexican food. The only means of redemption for this misdeed is a Mexican meal. Luckily, finding good Mexican grub in Phoenix is easy. Taco trucks are particularly fun to eat at because the experience feels authentic and honest—a modest kitchen packing a delicious punch. I was excited about trying Carte Blanche Gourmet Tacos, the allegedly amazing taco vending cart. It typically posts up at the Whole Foods parking lot in Scottsdale at Raintree Road and the 101 Freeway. The two tacos I ordered were loaded with portobello mushrooms, mozzarella cheese, and pumpkin seeds, an unexpected but delicious combination. Follow the truck on Twitter @tacochicks or check out www.facebook.com/pages/Carte-Blanche-Gourmet/146495075383157.

Frufru Pops, www.frufrupops.com. Once a month, Downtown Phoenix hosts First Friday in the trendy Roosevelt district and the popular art event doesn't break, even in the sweltering summer heat, which is exactly when I decided to go on the hunt for the

Frufru Pops food truck. Sure, I cursed myself a bit in the 100-degree (at night!) heat but once I realized that the pink and green logo on Frufru Pops's mobile *wasn't* a mirage, I was happy again. Frufru pops have easily the most untraditional, eccentric, and daring Popsicle flavors I have heard of. From honeydew-mint to cardamom-saffron yogurt, these pops will satisfy cravings you never knew you had. I savored every delicious ounce of the blood orange Popsicle and was so engulfed in its sweetness I forgot all about the heat. Follow the truck on Twitter @frufrupops or check out www.facebook.com/pages/Frufrupops/159499810765908.

Hey Joe! Filipino Street Food, (602) 410-8115; www.heyjoe truck.com. I think my favorite part about ordering food from a food stand or truck is the surprising originality in flavor I often find. Eating food prepared by chefs willing to hit the road and reach the people directly, peddling the food they lovingly cook on the streets, just makes my taste buds happy. I love knowing an up-and-coming home-style chef prepared my food. That's why I especially like Hey Joe! Filipino Street Food. If you're feeling adventurous try a chicken foot and eat the meat and skin right off the feet bones. Or, play it safe with *lumpia,* a Filipino deep-fried egg roll. Hey Joe! is a regular at the Downtown Phoenix Public Market's Food Truck Fridays. Follow the truck on Twitter @heyjoetruck or check out www.facebook.com/pages/Hey-Joe-Filipino-Street-Food-Truck/184512354929567.

Jamburritos, www.jamburritos.com. I know I know—Cajun food in Arizona? Impossible! Well, my friend, impossibility is nil. The

Jamburritos Cajun Grille Express truck is a large, white truck with rather intimidating letters and a nearly perfect rating on Yelp (again, conquering the impossible). The owners pride their cooking style on its Louisiana flavor without all those pesky calories and fats. Order the Jamburrito's namesake with Creole chicken, rice, andouille sausage, Cajun sauces, Pepper Jack cheese, and lettuce wrapped in a warm tortilla. (Okay, so they added a little Mexican flair to complement the Cajun cooking and woo the Phoenicians. Well, Jamburrito, mission accomplished.) Delicious! Follow the truck on Twitter @JamburritosKJUN or check out www.facebook.com/Jamburritos.

JP's Dog House, (480) 208-9353. Regardless of whether it's baseball season, sometimes a hot dog just sounds good. Ordering a hot dog out of a small vending cart under a bright red umbrella never gets old for your inner child, nor will imaginative condiments and top-pings above a juicy, succulent hot dog on a sweet, doughy bun. JP's Dog House is a very modest, down-to-earth hot dog stand with a killer summer special: goat cheese, grilled peaches and balsamic onions on a perfectly broiled jumbo hot dog. The food truck is a regular on the corner of Bethany Home Road and 15th Street in Phoenix.

Paradise Melts, (623) 229-2305; www.paradisemelts.com. As far as Paradise Melts is concerned, there is no such thing as over-the-top. From the electric blue Paradise Melts sandwich truck paint job to the mountain of fixings that come on your sandwich, you will quickly realize that subtlety is not the name of Paradise Melts's game. Like many good food trucks, Paradise Melts is a scrumptious option for anyone with a large appetite and no need for pretentious dining extravagance. The only frills you'll find here are in the sandwiches, like when the meat's juices soak into the warm bread's flaky crust, creating the perfect balance of soggy and crunchy with delicious flavors in between. The Reuben stacks pastrami, swiss cheese, coleslaw, and Thousand Island dressing a mile high between slices of marble rye bread. Eat it. Follow the truck on Twitter @paradisemelts or check out www.facebook.com/pages/paradise-melts/115711531778199.

Phoenix Cheesesteak Company, (480) 970-1102; www.phoenix cheesesteaks.com. Besides the first two letters of our cities' names, Phoenix and Philadelphia don't have a lot in common: The Diamondbacks always take a dive while the Phillies actually win sometimes and Philly freezes its buns off while Arizona enjoys its 60-degree winters. Phoenix Cheesesteak Company owner Ron Blom noticed a market in the Valley of the Sun for former East Coasters who miss their Philly cheesesteaks. He now serves 12-inch cheesesteak subs with rib eye steak, prepared in Southwest style for a little Phoenician flare. I loved the caramelized onions, peppers, portobello mushrooms, and avocado in the Westside Cheesesteak. Check them out on Facebook: www.facebook.com/PhoenixCheesesteaks.

Riteway Catering, (602) 448-3571; www.ritewaycatering.com. You'll be able to pick up the sweet aroma of barbecue sauce about 6 yards away from Riteway Catering Company's white and red 24-foot barbecue vending trailer. It may even tap your inner Warner Brothers Pepé Le Pew; my feet seem to float inches off the ground as soon as I get a whiff of the goods. Executive Chef Darryl King and Riteway Catering's trailer, a modern, mobile kitchen, specialize in catering private events and parties but vending delicious Southern food at other food truck gatherings is part of the gig, too. The Stuffed Chicken Scaloppine with wild mushroom and sage stuffing is a must-try. Follow the truck on Twitter @riteway catering or check out www.facebook.com/pages/Riteway-Catering-Company/131680986880045.

Short Leash Hot Dogs, (480) 620-8479; www.shortleashhotdogs .com. If you're coming from New York or Chicago, you may be a bit smug about your hot dogs. For a Southwestern spin on America's second-favorite fast food entree, try the mobile Short Leash Hot Dogs food truck, which specializes in Sonoran hot dogs. It's a large white truck with a sketch of a wiener dog on the side, so it's impossible to miss even in the sea of food trucks at Downtown Phoenix Public Market. Surprisingly, Short Leash Hot Dogs also has a healthy dose of vegetarian options so it's a good spot no matter what your food restrictions. In fact, the veggie dog with mango chutney and fried pickle was downright good. You can also order the hot dog in beef, pork, or chicken. Follow the truck on Twitter @shortleashdogs or check out www.facebook.com/shortleashhotdogs.

Sunshine and Spice, (602) 429-0800; www.sunshineandspice .com. For those of us who have never dealt with food allergies, we've been spared the exasperation of finding restaurants with food accommodating vegetarian-friendly or dairy- and gluten-free options. Fortunately, awareness is on the rise among the dining community, even when it comes to food trucks. Sunshine and Spice has a wide selection of goods, no matter what your food restrictions (or preference) might be. The vegan scramble is a good option if that's your bag with hot tofu, soyrizo (vegan chorizo) and spicy vegetable sauce, which packed a satisfying kick. Bring your pickiest eaters and let Sunshine and Spice worry about the rest. Follow the truck on Twitter @sun shinetruck or check out www.facebook.com/pages/ Sunshine-and-Spice/126367297410730.

Sweet Republic, (480) 248-6979; www.sweet republic.com. Sweet Republic ice cream is yours for the scooping at the Sweet Republic ice-cream shop in Scottsdale, ice-cream truck on the road, or in grocery stores all across the Valley of the Sun. Sweet Republic has made sure that you can satisfy your sweet tooth's sugary craving for Madagascar Vanilla, Salted Butter Caramel, or Brownie Swirl ice cream any time it sinks in. The Sweet Republic refurbished 1959 Chevy ice-cream truck, an orange homage to all that is funky, serves scoops of Sweet Republic's delicious "artisan" ice cream at First Friday in Phoenix or at the Old Town Scottsdale Farmers' Market. Follow the truck on Twitter @sweetrepublic or check out www.face book.com/sweetrepublic.

Tom's BBQ Pig Rig, (480) 464-0471; www.tomsbbq.com/PigRig .html. When you're ordering pizza, do you order triple pepperoni? Would you consider salad inadequate to qualify as dinner? Have you ever considered serving ribs at your wedding reception? Well, boy howdy, do I know a brilliant pink van you're going to love. Tom's BBQ Pig Rig has just about every type of barbecued meat you've ever dreamed of, served with 2 side dishes and dinner rolls. Think Southern picnic food, and forget about that diet you were thinking of starting. The pulled pork is delicious, and ordering out of a Pepto Bismol pink trunk is just plain fun. Follow the truck on Twitter @tomspigrig.

Torched Goodness, (480) 296-1609; www.torchedgoodness.com. As a food truck specializing in unique, original flavors of crème brûlée, Torched Goodness did not have to work very hard to win me over. The flavors on the menu included chocolate orange, coconut, s'mores, lavender, rose, lemon, caramel, and cappuccino. I chose the chocolate orange and spooned up a bite of the solidified, flavorful crème with the caramelized finish, a tasty combination of citrus and rich chocolate constituted in crème brûlée's creamy texture. I was also delighted to find out that the mobile restaurant serves local, fresh ingredients in its menu's meals, as well. Follow the truck on Twitter @torchedgoodness or check out www.face book.com/torchedgoodness.

Truckin' Good Food, (602) 492-2272; www.truckingoodfood .com. Truckin' Good Food sells Parisian street food that reflects the passionate beauty of the French capital itself, with an air of romance and rich flavors. Can you tell I practically fell in love with the melted hazelnut chocolate crepe? I would definitely recommend a sweet crepe (try bananas, walnuts, and Nutella) instead of a savory one if you'll only have time for one visit. And, regardless of how stuffed or broke you are, no trip to Truckin' Good Food is successful unless you order duck fat fries in curry mayo. Follow the truck on Twitter @truckingoodfood or check out www.facebook .com/TruckinGoodFood.

Phoenix & Scottsdale Food Glossary

Agave—Commonly known as the century plant, agave is a succulent that is found mostly in the Southwest as well as in Central and South America. There's a misconception that agave plants are cacti. Nor are they related to aloe, even though the two look similar. In Arizona's dining scene, agave nectar is often used as a healthier substitution to sugar. You'll find it in everything from desserts to cocktails.

Chimichanga—Also known as the food of the gods. Okay, maybe not, but I certainly can't resist this deep-fried burrito. It's popular in Southwestern, Tex-Mex, and Sonoran Mexican cuisine. Typically prepared with a flour tortilla, chimis can be stuffed with everything from shredded beef to shrimp and are often accompanied by salsa, sour cream, or guacamole. I like mine smothered, adding a layer of green or red sauce on top.

Chipotle—No, not the McDonald's-owned fast food chain. We're talking about the smoke-fried jalapeño that's used in Mexican and Mexican-inspired food. Most of these spicy little firecrackers are produced in the Mexican state of Chihuahua. On the local dining scene, they're used to spice up all kinds of food dishes and also are incorporated into things like mayonnaise, ketchup, and other sauces for an extra kick.

Churro—Occasionally, you'll hear the *churro* referred to as a Spanish doughnut. It makes sense given that it's a fried pastry treat popular in Arizona's Mexican and Southwestern restaurants for dessert. Interestingly, the *churro* is actually a breakfast meal in places like Mexico and Spain. No matter: In both instances they're served with hot chocolate or *café con leche* for dipping. And that's all that matters.

Fry bread—Fry bread is a flat dough circle that's deep fried in oil and can be eaten as a savory meal, with toppings like chicken, cheese, and hot sauce (also known as a Navajo taco), or as a sweet delight when it's coated in powdered sugar and drizzled in honey. Both are worth the calories and can be found at festivals and fairs in Greater Phoenix and Scottsdale, as well as the Fry Bread House near Downtown Phoenix.

Habanero—Listen here, gringo, just because you can stomach a jalapeño doesn't mean you should dive into a jar of habanero chili peppers. Got it? These zesty orange-red bulbs are among the spiciest peppers around, with a Scoville scale rating measuring between 100,000 and 350,000 on average. Like its other pepper family members, the habanero can be used as spice in sauces and broths, or served chopped in rice, beans, salad—just about anything you can imagine.

Machaca—You can thank the cowboys and ranchers of Northern Mexico for *machaca*, dried and spiced meat (usually beef) that's rehydrated, then pounded to make it tender. It's cooked in a mixture of its own juices and spices for a slightly piquant flavor then used in everything from tacos to burritos and flautas. One of my favorite forms is the breakfast dish that scrambles *machaca* with eggs and peppers.

Mole—In Mexico and other Spanish-speaking countries, *mole* is a generic term for a variety of different sauces. In restaurants across Greater Phoenix and Scottsdale, *mole* often refers to the specific *"mole poblano,"* or a deep red sauce made from spicy poblano peppers. It's a very rich, bold sauce that typically accompanies some kind of chicken dish.

New Mexican food—New Mexican cuisine combines techniques and flavors from Native American, Mexican, Spanish, and United States cultures. While it's most popular in other Southwestern states like California and Nevada, there are places across Arizona that feature its dishes based around New Mexican chiles, blue corn, and *sopapillas*.

Pepita—This one's easy. A *pepita* is just the Spanish word for pumpkin seed. You can roast them whole for a delicious salty snack or toast them and throw into salads and side dishes for a crunchy texture. *Pepitas* also are oftentimes used in *mole* dishes.

Prickly Pear—The prickly pear cactus produces a bright pink fruit at the very tip of its paddle-shaped arm. When carefully peeled and de-spined, these "cactus figs" can be enjoyed roasted and whole or made into jam, jelly, lemonade, candy, and even margaritas and vodka! Restaurants across Arizona often use prickly pear in Southwestern-influenced dishes and menus.

Serrano—On the spicy scale, serrano peppers fall somewhere in between jalapeños and habaneros. They have a crisp, bright (but biting!) flavor and look like a red version of their jalapeño cousins. Serrano peppers are usually eaten raw and oftentimes used in fresh *pico de gallo* salsa. Serrano peppers are among the most commonly used peppers in Mexico, too.

Sonoran Hot Dog—You've had a chili dog, right? Well, a Sonoran hot dog is basically a chili dog, on steroids. These bacon-wrapped dogs are blanketed in a soft Mexican roll then topped with pinto beans, onions, tomatoes, jalapeño sauce, cheese, mayo, ketchup, and mustard. Usually, they're served with a roasted chile on the side and occasionally with green onion.

Sopapilla—You could compare the *sopapilla* to fry bread, though it's more diamond-shaped and less dense. It's also more commonly served as a dessert dish sandwiching a healthy drizzle of honey and anything else the restaurant can dream up. There are a few restaurants, though, that will serve it as a savory main dish stuffed with meat and cheese.

Street Corn—Google recipes for street corn and you'll get endless pages of results. In my opinion, this dish is best kept to its humble beginnings: with a spread of Mexican crème and lightly dusted with cayenne pepper, Cotija cheese, and lime. Street corn got its start with Mexican street vendors and is now popular in Valley of the Sun restaurants like **Gallo Blanco Cafe & Bar** (see p. 76).

Street Tacos—Like street corn, street tacos got their start with Mexican vendors and are an off-the-cart, simpler version of corn tortillas stuffed with beef or pork. At most, they are served with *pico de gallo* or salsa. No cabbage, lettuce, tomatoes, or dressing here: just flavorful meat and salsa.

Tex Mex—Tex Mex is a localized version of Mexican food that blends products found in the United States with traditional Mexican dishes. Typically, Tex Mex flavors are more tame than Mexican (or, in my opinion, bland) and the rice is often served with peas, another no-no in my book. But, hey, some restaurants in Greater Phoenix and Scottsdale actually do Tex Mex well, like Spotted Donkey.

Tequila and Mescal—Tequila is actually a type of mescal (also written *mezcal*), which is an all-encompassing term for any liquor made from the agave plant. "Real" tequila is produced in the Jalisco state of Mexico and made from blue agave. Its process is very strictly regulated. Mescal, meanwhile, is made in different areas of Mexico and from a variety of agave plants. In general, mescal has a smokier flavor than tequila.

Tomatillo—The tomatillo looks like a mini green tomato and is a staple in Mexican cuisine. It's a small fruit that's enveloped by a paper-thin husk. Tomatillos are used in many Mexican sauces, and are especially popular in making mild green salsa. They also are sometimes used to make jams and other sweet preserves.

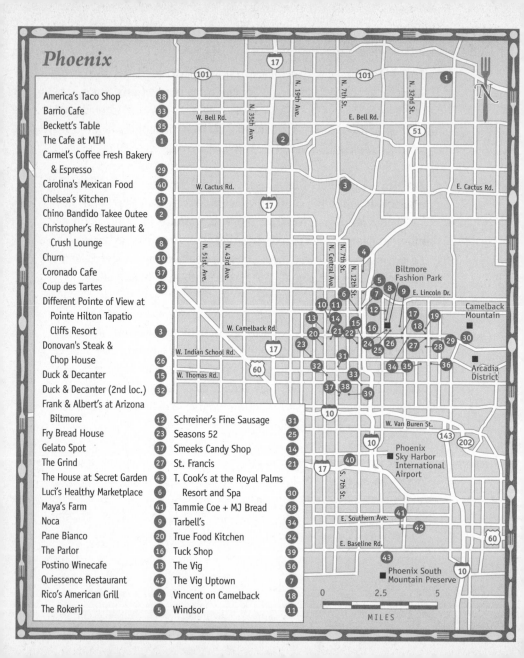

Phoenix

Phoenix

This is where things might get a little complicated, so stick with me. The City of Phoenix proper is Arizona's capital and the sixth largest city in the United States. Greater Phoenix is an all-encompassing term used to reference the City of Phoenix and all of its surrounding municipalities, like Glendale, Chandler, Tempe, and even Scottsdale. You'll also hear people refer to Greater Phoenix as the Valley of the Sun for one very obvious reason: 300 plus days of sunshine per year. In this book, I've separated Phoenix proper into its own section in hopes of doing its dynamic dining scene some justice.

Because Phoenix is a relatively new city by United States standards—it was officially recognized in 1868—it seems to carry a reputation of being a place void of the culture and dining repertoire more "established" places like New York and San Francisco are constantly touting. I can't emphasize enough how untrue this assumption is. Long before any cowboy settled the Wild West, Phoenix was inhabited by a forward-thinking Native American tribe, called the Hohokam, who made water readily available in the Sonoran Desert with a series of ancient canals that are still in operation across the

Valley of the Sun today. It was this enterprising mentality that laid the foundation for Phoenix agriculture, an industry that spurred its development.

Like the Greater Phoenix Convention & Visitors Bureau website proclaims, "things are different in the desert. The sky is bigger. The stars are brighter. The sunsets stop you in your tracks." And while the sunsets certainly are beyond words, it's the local restaurant and chef community that is catching the attention of discerning palates across the globe. Passionate foodies far and wide travel to Phoenix for a taste of Barrio Cafe's Southwestern staples, or Quiessence Restaurant's daily menu with its farm-fresh produce. They've read about people like Christopher Gross and Mark Tarbell in their *Food & Wines* and *Bon Appétits,* and now they want to try the real thing.

So, I'm just going to come right out and say it: Phoenix doesn't need to compete with the Los Angeleses or Miamis of the world, because we have a high caliber of gastronomic masters right here at home that keeps us on top of our game. We're not trying to top Chicago or outdo San Francisco. We're just here, doing our thing in the laid-back Southwest, enjoying the sunshine and the good earthly stuff that comes with it. Do we hope you enjoy it? Of course. Will it break our hearts if you don't? Probably not. But give us a shot and we're willing to bet that you won't go home hungry.

America's Taco Shop, 2041 N. 7th St., Phoenix, AZ 85006; (602) 682-5627; www.americastacoshop.net; Mexican; $. You'll feel like you've stepped into a Baja roadside stand when you visit any of America's Taco Shop's locations. The culinary gems are set up in brightly colored beach bungalow-style homes and attract throngs of customers daily with authentic street tacos. These tasty creations come in 2 flavors: traditional *carne asada* (beef) and *al pastor* (pork), which is a fantastic combination of sweet and spicy with chunks of pineapple and a snappy tomato salsa. America's Taco Shop is a trip down Nostalgia Boulevard with glass-bottled Coca-Cola and its sweeter "MexiCoke" brother, made with refined cane sugar instead of corn syrup like in the United States. Order one of the homemade *agua frescas*, Mexican fresh fruit drinks, and kick back on the outdoor patio. And stay. For as many meals as humanly possible. There is a second location at 4447 N. 7th Ave., Phoenix, AZ 85013; (602) 515-0856 and a third location at 735 E. University Dr., Tempe, AZ 85281; (480) 751-6250.

Barrio Cafe, 2814 N. 16th St., Phoenix, AZ 85006; (602) 636-0240; www.barriocafe.com; Mexican; $$$. Chef Silvana Salcido Esparza, whose parents owned and operated the first and only Mexican bakery in Merced, California, grew up surrounded by food, but her culinary roots date back even further than childhood. In fact, the family cooking history got its start in the 1200s when the

All-Star & Celebrity Chefs: Silvana Salcido Esparza

Silvana Salcido Esparza of **Barrio Cafe** taught us the difference between Mexican food and Mexican cuisine, the latter of which is as complex and refined as French fine dining. Esparza draws on her formal culinary training and travels throughout Mexico, where she seeks out recipes that are worth the spotlight in Greater Phoenix and Scottsdale's dining scene. She focuses on regional Mexican dishes like *cochinita pibil*, a Yucatan specialty of citrus-marinated pork spiked with achiote, an earthy Mexican spice. Esparza proves that south-of-the-border dining isn't all about burritos and gloppy cheese.

"el Salcidos" worked as royal pastry chefs to King Alonso El Sabio of Spain. True story. History repeats itself in the best possible way at Barrio Cafe where Esparza works her magic on dishes like *Filete de mi Tita*, grilled filet topped with Mexican style crab and ancho chile sauce, and the gooiest but most sophisticated *chile relleno* you'll ever try. The poblano pepper is stuffed with shrimp and scallops, then topped with a blend of fontina and Oaxaca Mexican cheeses.

Beckett's Table, 3717 E. Indian School Rd., Phoenix, AZ 85018; (602) 954-1700; www.beckettstable.com; American; $$. A few years ago, Chef Justin Beckett was heading up the kitchen at a restaurant where the vibe was all about "fashionable" food and the menu had a $30 sandwich. The recession forced the establishment to close its doors, and, I'm not exaggerating when I say this, Phoenix foodies mourned the loss of Chef Beckett's skills. (Even though they didn't give a rip about saying goodbye to the overpriced menu.) But that's all fine because Beckett is now where he belongs: running shop and the kitchen at Beckett's Table in Phoenix's Arcadia District where the rock-shrimp enchiladas, matzo ball soup, and fire-roasted green chile pork stew are enough to erase that lobster-something-or-other sandwich from the food history books. If you're traveling with the family and tired of eating at chain restaurants for the sake of affordable prices and kid-approved options, Beckett's Table is a breath of fresh air. The "Tobin Kids Menu," named after Chef's son, has a slew of tasty child-friendly items like grilled chicken skewers and pasta n' red sauce. See Chef Beckett's recipe for **Creamy Grits n' Sausage** on p. 240.

The Cafe at MIM, 4725 E. Mayo Blvd., Phoenix, AZ 85050; (480) 478-6000; www.themim.org; Cafe Fare; $. I was so surprised by the Cafe at MIM's rave reviews from Phoenix's toughest food critic that I had to go and check it out myself. I mean, it's a cafe. At a museum. Could it really be worth the 4 out of 5 stars from a guy who makes even the boldest chefs in town sweat? Short answer: yes. While it has a cafeteria setup, complete with slide-and-go trays, the Cafe at MIM reminds me more of an airy California bistro than a high-school lunchroom. Its food is much more advanced, too, with a daily-changing menu from Bon Appétit, a company that runs similar services for museums like the Getty Center in Los Angeles. I melted over a rich butternut squash soup with spiced sunflower seeds to start, and then was drawn to the pork osso bucco because of its use of local purveyors Wilson Ranch and Seacat Gardens. Thankfully, my dining partner took my not-so-subtle suggestions and ordered the day's pizza. It was made with roasted nantes carrots, marjoram, and feta. Delicious. If you have any dietary restrictions, you'll appreciate the Cafe at MIM for its color-coded menu that designates vegetarian- and celiac-friendly dishes.

Chelsea's Kitchen, 5040 N. 40th St., Phoenix, AZ 85018; (602) 957-2555; www.chelseaskitchenaz.com; American; $$. Vegetarians love Chelsea's Kitchen because of its wide selection of non-meat menu items, with two of the most popular dishes being the Brussels Sprouts Salad (a coleslaw-like concoction with dried cranberries, blueberries, almonds, and tangy mustard vinaigrette) and the vegetarian taco plate with locally farmed, seasonal vegetables. What keeps me coming back is the not-so-vegetarian Angus beef Chelsea's Cheeseburger and its perfectly piquant Russian dressing. CK's weekend brunch menu also is popular with locals who flock to the trendy Arcadia restaurant like flies to sugar for a taste of *chilaquiles* with chicken, egg, and ranchero sauce, or hotcakes with homemade maple syrup.

Chino Bandido Takee Outee, 15414 N. 19th Ave., Ste. K, Phoenix, AZ 85032; (602) 375-3639; www.chinobandido.com; Fusion; $. Chino Bandido probably won't be winning any *Food & Wine* awards any time soon, but it's every Phoenix foodie's favorite guilty pleasure. A fusion of Chinese and Mexican cuisine, Chino Bandido is the brainchild of area residents Frank and Eve Collins, and combines Eve's Chinese ancestry with the couple's love for Mexican food. The decor at this ultra casual restaurant is exactly that, but the menu will bring out your quirkiest cravings. The ordering process can seem confusing at first but works like this: Select your base and put its corresponding number in the first box. A number alone means you'll get that item—Chinese BBQ pork, menu item #3, for example—over a bowl of steamed white rice. Want it in a burrito? Write down 3B. Eyeing the quesadilla? That's 3Q.

Christopher's Restaurant & Crush Lounge, 2502 E. Camelback Rd., Ste. 102, Phoenix, AZ 85016; (602) 522-2344; www.christophers az.com; Fusion; $$$. Hometown hero Christopher Gross got his start in the industry as a janitor in restaurant kitchens across Phoenix, and is today the chef and owner of what is considered one of the city's best fine dining spots. His international training in London and Paris was well worth the travel expense, because the smoked truffle filet mignon at Christopher's was one of those

All-Star & Celebrity Chefs: Christopher Gross

Christopher Gross is seen as a hometown hero because he learned the culinary arts in Los Angeles, London, and Paris, and then returned to Phoenix, where he grew up. Within a few years, he turned a town of steakhouse fanatics into fine dining connoisseurs. Soon, everyone was obsessed with restaurants using quality ingredients and this extended into personal kitchens, too. People ditched ready-made frozen meals and ingredients for actual meat, vegetables, and ground spices. Eventually, Gross opened his namesake restaurant in Phoenix and introduced another novel concept: a multi-course tasting menu where the food is the main event.

"I'm never going to forget this meal for as long as I live" moments. The charbroiled flavor was brought out even more by its truffle oil drizzle. For lunch, a more affordable option is the express menu. It is a 3-course, prix-fixe meal for $20, not including tax and tip. Obviously not as wallet-friendly as your favorite fast food haunt (you know you have one), but a great way to sample some of Phoenix's best gourmet food for a relatively cheaper price.

Coronado Cafe, 2201 N. 7th St., Phoenix, AZ 85006; (602) 258-5149; www.coronadocafe.com; Cafe Fare; $$. If I had to give one place on this list the "Cutest Restaurant Award," it would be Coronado Cafe, mostly because of its charming exterior. Coronado Cafe makes its home, quite literally, in a renovated Arizona 1930s-era house decked with green, red, and yellow trimmings. But this pretty little eatery is actually a restaurant *femme fatale*. Sure, the menu does have typical "cafe" food like sandwiches and salads, but it's also much more robust with atypical featured entrees like rigatoni white meat Bolognese and roasted vegetable and chevre *rellenos*. Even the hummus takes an interesting spin with studded pomegranate seeds and roasted serrano chiles.

Donovan's Steak & Chop House, 3101 E. Camelback Rd., Phoenix, AZ 85016; (602) 955-3666; www.donovanssteakhouse .com; Steakhouse; $$$. Donovan's Steak & Chop House is everything your dad would ever want from a steakhouse: a dining room full of private booths, mahogany furniture, and bronze sculptures. Luckily, the food is everything you'd ever want from one, too: USDA prime beef alongside seasonal vegetables, fresh seafood, and pork and veal chops. Filet mignon, peppercorn filets, and New York strips are available in a range of sizes, and the Classic Entrees menu includes your choice of steak plus potato (everything from au gratin to garlic mashed) and vegetable, all for one base price.

If you're not in the mood for steak, try the Australian rock lobster tail, which is broiled, sweet, and tender, or the Alaskan red king crab legs. From 4 to 6 p.m. Mon through Fri, Donovan's gives out complimentary prime filet steak mini-sandwiches for happy hour. Yes, for free. Order from the long list of specialty martinis and kick back for a few hours. Oh, and if you're a wine lover, here's a little tip: The bartenders are extra generous on the pours.

Frank & Albert's at Arizona Biltmore, 2400 E. Missouri Ave., Phoenix, AZ 85016; (602) 381-7632; www.frankandalberts.com; American; $$$. Named after Frank Lloyd Wright and Albert Chase McArthur, who designed the Arizona Biltmore Resort, Frank & Albert's is a fairly new concept, having opened in the fall of 2009. Chefs Todd Sicolo and Conor Favre put Wright's concept of organic architecture to work with a culinary spin, sourcing peaches, goat cheese, balsamic vinegar, and more from area farms like Black Mesa Ranch and Windmill. I was drawn to the pork chops with caramelized apples, mostly because the chops were cooked with Coca-Cola, and was glad I indulged my childhood nostalgia for the evening. Frank & Albert's also has an entire section of their dessert menu dedicated to the "ooey and gooey" with treats like tableside s'mores; mudslide pie; and the Shaken, Rattled, and Rolled, which is basically fried dough topped with powdered sugar and prickly pear honey. It's messy, but worth it.

The Grind, 3961 E. Camelback Rd., Phoenix, AZ 85018; (602) 954-7463; www.thegrindaz.com; Hamburgers; $$. *Bon Appétit* magazine named the Grind as one of the country's Top 10 Best New Burger Spots. This, coupled with their 1,000-degree coal-burning oven, piqued my interest enough to set a date with a friend the very next day. Apparently, this tricked-out oven is supposed to help seal in the meat's juiciness and create a flavorful outer crust. I am happy to say, the reports were true. Because this is a book about Arizona, I couldn't pass on the opportunity to try the Nogales Burger, where the patty is actually topped with a flattened chorizo tamale. It was a lot, but it was more than good, especially with the slight kick from the roasted poblano pepper and white cheddar cheese. Other highlights included the Texas sake-fed Kobe burger with shiitake tempura and the Sweet and Spicy burger jazzed up with candied jalapeños and fried ratatouille. Important to note is the fact that the Grind only uses locally grown organic vegetables for their toppings and sides, and that there wasn't a toned-down children's menu so it's definitely a "grown up" hamburger spot.

The House at Secret Garden, 2501 E. Baseline Rd., Phoenix, AZ 85042; (602) 243-8539; www.houseatsecretgarden.com; American; $$. The House at Secret Garden is one of the best places for alfresco patio dining in Phoenix because it is nestled right onto the side of South Mountain and lined by stunning gardens and stately trees. Couple that with a sunset and the fact that it's housed in an old Spanish mansion, and you've got yourself a very romantic meal. There's a wide selection of appetizers with portions perfect for sharing, soups and salads, and hearty mains like osso bucco and homemade pasta. The menu here changes regularly but we were lucky enough to get our hands on the roasted cauliflower soup, made from McClendon Farms cauliflower, fresh mint, and toasted bread crumbs that I would buy by the pound. The handmade pasta that day was delicious spinach ravioli stuffed with halibut and leeks in lemon sauce.

Noca, 3118 E. Camelback Rd., Phoenix, AZ 85016; (602) 956-6622; www.restaurantnoca.com; American; $$$. Never mind the fact that Noca is located in a strip mall. Never mind the fact that it's next to a grocery store and that it has a pasta dish on the menu that's priced at $19. If you are planning one "special treat" excursion when you are in Phoenix, let Noca be it. Do yourself a favor: Order the Maine Lobster Roll with 2, count 'em 2, different kinds of aioli (they're roasted garlic and smoked paprika), and celery root, lime, and a delicious blend of herbs. Also a highlight was the handmade pastas and, for the main event, a monkfish with a parsnip puree that I am surprised I enjoyed so much. Be warned, though. For such a beautiful restaurant, Noca's patio isn't much to see and faces the grocery store parking lot.

Pane Bianco, 4404 N. Central Ave., Ste. A, Phoenix, AZ 85012; (602) 234-2100; www.pizzeriabianco.com/pane; Sandwiches; $$. The more simplistic sister restaurant to Pizzeria Bianco, Pane Bianco is a takeout-only spot where you've got exactly 4 sandwich choices: caprese; tuna with red onion, olives, lemon, and arugula; soppressata with aged provolone and roasted peppers; and the daily market sandwich. It's the epitome of sweet and simple. My personal favorite, the soppressata, comes on the house flatbread (the perfect combination of crispy and chewy) with shaved Parmesan on top of the provolone—which, you know, I didn't necessarily object about—and sweet roasted red peppers. There is a small selection of salads, too, which are basically non-breaded versions of the sandwiches. There's a very limited amount of outdoor seating so I recommend grabbing lunch and walking the couple blocks east to Indian Steele Park on 7th Street.

The Parlor, 1916 E. Camelback Rd., Phoenix, AZ 85016; (602) 248-2480; www.theparlor.us; Italian; $$. Owner Aric Mei knows a thing or two about pizza, especially considering his father and three uncles founded **Nello's**, the long-running local pizzeria franchise. While the Parlor's pies are more European and artisanal than the Chicago style of Nello's, Mei did take a note or two from his family in terms of pricing. Prices at the Parlor are definitely reasonable and they also give you the option of ordering half-sized portions of pretty much everything on the menu at reduced cost!

The bruschetta at the Parlor is more than above average but what really stood out on our visit was the arancini—crispy-fried risotto balls stuffed with rice and Parmesan cheese. They're topped with a flavorful red tomato sauce that you'll dream about. Brick oven pizzas here range from the rich puttanesca with calamari, rock shrimp, capers, and spicy tomato sauce to the lighter, more traditional Margherita drizzled with an extra virgin olive oil. There's also homemade pasta and a respectable cocktail list.

Quiessence Restaurant at the Farm at South Mountain, 6106 S. 32nd St., Phoenix, AZ 85042; (602) 276-0601; www.quies sencerestaurant.com; American; $$$. Quiessence Restaurant is one of three dining destinations at the Farm at South Mountain and many of its ingredients come from Maya's Farm, a smaller sustainable garden and market that sits on the same 12 acres of pecan groves as the restaurant. It's also one of the most popular alfresco dining retreats in all of Greater Phoenix and Scottsdale, so scoring a table during the prime winter and spring months can be a challenge. Make a reservation and then indulge in its daily-changing menu of house-cured salami, artisan cheese, and prime meat and seafood. Dessert also varies with each visit, but I struck gold one night with the Confectioner's Plate, a sweet smorgasbord of whoopie pies, milk chocolate lime truffles, bowtie pecan turtles, and iced chocolate milk with whipped cream.

Rico's American Grill, 7677 N. 16th St., Phoenix, AZ 85020; (602) 997-5850; www.ricosag.com; Southwestern; $$$. Rico's American Grill is a great casual place to go for affordable bar food that doesn't taste like a cocktail waitress made it. Happy Hour at Rico's goes until 7 p.m. and is definitely a draw with half-off appetizers like the Shrimp Corn Dogs, jumbo shrimp served with Old Bay remoulade sauce, and Mini Dogs & Fixin's, with Rico's Rough Rider Brew mustard. The beer is a signature item at Rico's. For dinner, the flatbreads are good, but mostly taste just like any other flatbread, so not necessarily worth the $12+ price tag. The fish tacos with fire-roasted salsa and black beans were definitely above average, and the Wicked Meatloaf with mashed potatoes and cracked pepper demi-glaze is as fun as it sounds. I like Rico's because it doesn't try too hard. The food is straightforward and good, self-parking is abundant (a commodity in valet-obsessed Greater Phoenix), and the menu is easy to navigate. Side note: Rico's also has free wireless access so it's convenient if you are a business traveler, too.

The Rokerij, 6335 N. 16th St., Phoenix, AZ 85016; (602) 287-8900; www.burningembersphoenix.com; Steakhouse; $$. Rokerij is a Dutch word for "smokehouse" and that's exactly what this restaurant was originally modeled after with its dark and cozy (some might even say romantic) atmosphere. The Rokerij has since evolved into what would technically be classified as an American steakhouse, but I find it to be so much more. If you are a fan of shellfish, start with the Oysters Rokerij with spinach, Dungeness crab, crumbled bacon, and a rich but spicy bacon and jalapeño hollandaise. The chicken schnitzel is moist and flavorful with a buttery lemon caper sauce that sops the porous tagliatelle pasta in a wonderful way. I'm reminded of blissful meals back home in Croatia with the Mixed Grill entree, which is a very European-style dish with 3 kinds of meat; lamb chop, beef, and pork tenderloin. It's served with 3 different sauces, veggies, and either potatoes or pasta.

Seasons 52, 2502 E. Camelback Rd., Phoenix, AZ 85016; (602) 840-5252; www.seasons52.com; American; $$. While it's a larger franchise restaurant and not a homegrown treat, I was still intrigued by Seasons 52 because nothing on the menu is more than 475 calories. Naturally, I assumed this just meant bite-sized portions but I was pleasantly surprised to find that the low calorie count is thanks to the fresh, seasonal ingredients and not because they're stingy on serving sizes. There on a lunch date with a friend, we swooned over the Sonoma goat cheese ravioli with vegetables, roasted garlic, and fresh basil in a light tomato broth. Grilled pineapple on the spicy chipotle shrimp flatbread was a nice touch to the feta cheese and poblano peppers, too. Desserts at Seasons 52 are served in shot glasses and, while small, pack a flavorful punch—especially the chocolate peanut butter mousse. I wonder if there comes a point where you eat so much that the whole "475 calories" thing becomes irrelevant? I might be open to testing that.

St. Francis, 111 E. Camelback Rd., Phoenix, AZ 85012; (602) 200-8111; www.stfrancisaz.com; American; $$. The architecture at St. Francis is as much of a reason to visit as the food. Housed in a 1950s-era building that was once a bank, the restaurant's design is clean and modern, and makes fantastic use of brick, wood, and glass texture to produce a vibe that is all at once edgy and warm. Minimalist stainless steel tables, a multicolored chalkboard menu, and large roll-up door that turns the restaurant into an indoor/outdoor space in nice weather, give St. Francis a trendy and urban attitude that doesn't feel forced. It is edgy but hospitable. St. Francis is all about wood-fired, seasonal food and simple flavors, and the crisp on the outside, chewy on the inside brick oven bread is tied for my vote for best in town. Having worked for big names like Jean-Georges Vongerichten and Michael Richard, Chef Aaron Chamberlin delivers with his solid, honest-to-goodness dishes like roasted chicken with parsnip, broccolini, and pomegranate in garlic sauce. The Forbidden Rice Bowl is a favorite too, with 7 ever-changing seasonal vegetables, ginger, garlic, and a sweet and spicy dressing that I wish they would sell by the trough. And while, typically, a flatbread is a flatbread (is a flatbread), the fluffy versions at St. Francis are definite standouts. Try the smoked salmon with lemon, dill, capers, and crème fraîche. See Chef Chamberlin's recipe for **Sticky Toffee Pudding** on p. 252.

T. Cook's at the Royal Palms Resort and Spa, 5200 E. Camelback Rd., Phoenix, AZ 85018; (602) 808-0766; www.royal palmshotel.com; Mediterranean; $$$. Its location at the Spanish

Colonial–inspired Royal Palms Resort and Spa, originally built in 1929 as a summer retreat for a wealthy financier, gives T. Cook's an exotic appeal that will make you swear you are somewhere in the Mediterranean, save for the sweeping views of Phoenix's iconic Camelback Mountain. The food at T. Cook's plays off this theme with dishes like pan-roasted sole stuffed with an onion marmalade and served with whole grain mustard that absolutely pops with flavor. The paella is hearty and delicious on its own, but even better with the buttery lobster tail add-on. Sunday brunch at T. Cook's has become somewhat of a Phoenix tradition. From the entree list, highlights include the lemon brioche French toast and Mediterranean eggs Benedict, but I love going with the Market Buffet option because of the wide selection of items like fruit, cheese, crab legs, fresh salads, and more.

True Food Kitchen, 2502 E. Camelback Rd., Ste. 135, Phoenix, AZ 85016; (602) 774-3488; www.truefoodkitchen.com; Fusion; $$. A partnership between Dr. Andrew Weil and local boy/restaurant industry mogul Sam Fox, True Food Kitchen makes eating healthy an unexpected treat with a menu that focuses more on sustainable and organic food than it does calorie-counting. It's packed with nutritious vegetables, whole grains, and lean proteins that are all mashed together in a variety of tasty ways. The Tuscan kale salad is a dependable go-to with a Parmesan bread-crumb topping that you'll dream about for days afterward, and the wasabi aioli on the ahi tuna sliders makes them a must-try as well. Other crowd pleasers on our visit were the miso glazed black cod, and the edamame dumplings drizzled in white truffle oil for a very rich and satisfying flavor. The cocktail list at True Food Kitchen is fun, too, with a light and refreshing lineup. I loved the Red Moon with pink grapefruit juice, yuzu, agave, and soda. There's a second True Food Kitchen location at 15191 N. Scottsdale Rd., Ste. 100, Scottsdale, AZ 85254; (480) 265-4500.

Tuck Shop, 2245 N. 12th St., Phoenix, AZ 85006; (602) 354-2980; www.tuckinphx.com; Wine Bar; $$. Tucked away in Phoenix's Coronado neighborhood in a '50s-era building, the Tuck Shop is a favorite among locals who sit back in the mid-century living room setting for meals of medjool dates stuffed with Schreiner's chorizo and citrus-brined chicken with white cheddar waffles. In fact, the Tuck Shop practically encourages you to stay awhile and has shelves stocked with books, magazines, games, and toys. A tip: Always add the "lobstah" when ordering the Times Mac and Cheese and don't miss out on the Chicory Salad with hazelnuts, roasted squash, endive, and a fantastic desert honey–chestnut buttermilk dressing.

The Vig, 4041 N. 40th St., Phoenix, AZ 85018; (602) 553-7227; www.thevigus.com; Gastropub; $$. The Vig is a tavern in the sense that it is a popular neighborhood watering hole, but it also happens

HOME GROWN CHAINS: TWO HIPPIES MAGIC MUSHROOM BURGERS

Dying to wear your hippie-style round glasses with metal frames and pink lenses? Tired of strangers glancing disapprovingly at your frayed cutoffs, but not in the mood to give peas a chance? Well, reader, welcome home. **Two Hippies Magic Mushroom Burgers** (www .twohippiesburgers.com) is a hippie haven for all your greasy, delicious, American fast food favorites. If you're not in the mood to try this far-out joint's namesake (though every bite of these burgers drips with savory beefy goodness), try their charbroiled hot dog, recipient of *Phoenix New Times* magazine's "Best Hot Dog" title in 2009.

to serve some killer food. But it doesn't have the cavernous, hole-in-the-wall atmosphere that is associated with the term. Yes, the lighting is dim and the wood finishing is dark, but the Vig is much swankier than your run-of-the-mill tavern. On any given night, it is packed with a mix of Phoenix hipsters, professionals, and area college students who come for the bocce ball, live music, and consistently good food. I love the Hot Vings (my favorite are the Thai sweet chili), VigAzz Burger on a pretzel bun (always add the fried egg), and the Not So Nachos with slow roasted pork, white cheddar, green onions, and their homemade tortilla chips. Locals dig the Vig because of the amazing weekly specials. By far the most popular is "Sunday School" with half-priced bottles (that's bottles, not glasses) of wine and live music from local bands. There's also a location at 6015 N. 16th St., Phoenix, AZ 85014; (602) 633-1187.

Windsor, 5223 N. Central Ave., Phoenix, AZ 85012; (602) 279-1111; www.windsoraz.com; Gastropub; $$. Windsor is one of the newest concepts from **Postino Winecafe** owner Craig DeMarco. It shares the same renovated 1940s building as **Churn** (an ice-cream shop and also new from DeMarco) and features what the owner calls "glorified bar food." I didn't have the heart to break it to DeMarco that "glorified" has negative connotations and is used to describe something that is overestimated, so I'll make it up by telling you that Windsor is, in fact, worth the hype. Its all-day menu is accessible, casual, and family friendly with a kids' section that's only $5 for a main, side, and drink. Grown-ups will find starters like corn dog poppers, picnic kebabs, and—my favorite—the Smorgasbord. It is $10 for a plate of house smoked salmon, kale chips, pickled vegetables, bean dip, grilled pita, cheese, and mixed nuts. There's a list of salads, everything from kale Caesar to Waldorf chicken, and main dishes consist of a selection of sandwiches like the *banh mi* halibut with honey soy glaze, carrots, cucumber, cilantro, and spicy chili sauce. Desserts include homemade doughnuts with chocolate fudge and jam, and a milk chocolate tart with peanut and pretzel crust.

Carolina's Mexican Food, 1202 E. Mohave St., Phoenix, AZ 85034; (602) 252-1503; www.carolinasmex.com; Mexican; $. Every city has them: those inconspicuous restaurants where the aesthetics toe the line between authentic and grungy, but every local swears by the grits or ribs, or, in the case of Carolina's Mexican Food, the chimichanga, tamales, tostadas, burros, and just about everything else on the menu. The outside of its original location looks more like a warehouse than a restaurant but inside is a gastronomical goldmine waiting to be discovered. Carolina's serves breakfast, lunch, and dinner, and has a long list of everything from three-way red chili beef burros to simple bean tostadas and chicken *flautas* (rolled tacos). Opened in 1968, Carolina's has become a Phoenix dining institution. Stop by for a weekday lunch and you're bound to see a mixture of the Phoenix business crowd, construction workers, and even city mayors and police officials. There is a second location at 2126 E. Cactus Rd., Phoenix, AZ 85022; (602) 275-8231.

Coup des Tartes, 4626 N. 16th St., Phoenix, AZ 85016; (602) 212-1082; www.nicetartes.com; French; $$$. Coup des Tartes is Arizona's longest running BYOB restaurant and a favorite of couples, who love to canoodle over pâté and brûlée in the restaurant's candlelit white tablecloth setting. I was impressed by the looks of the cheese plate and drooled over the idea of munching on nutty Italian Parmigiano and French Brillat-Savarin, but instead opted for the Three Onion Tarte, which was satisfyingly sweet and flaky with caramelized shallots and earthy gruyère. Even though the tart came with mixed greens, the roasted apples and toasted hazelnuts on the Roquefort salad sounded too good not to try, especially since it came with dried figs and a Premier Cru dressing. My companion, who loves duck, told me that the duck breast entree was juicy and wonderful. I'm not a fan of the meat, but I did appreciate the slightly honeyed acidity of the blood orange glaze with the basmati rice. But I got much more of a kick from the lobster with orange-apple chutney and a creamy risotto.

Different Pointe of View at Pointe Hilton Tapatio Cliffs Resort, 11111 N. 7th St., Phoenix, AZ 85020; (602) 866-6350; www.tapatiocliffshilton.com; American; $$$. The vistas granted by its careful positioning at the top of North Mountain in Phoenix are what have kept Different Pointe of View at the top of the local food chain for more than 25 years. Even as new spots pop up in equally stunning environments across Greater Phoenix and Scottsdale, you will still be hard pressed to find a view that beats this one. Floor-to-ceiling windows mean you'll get the effect from anywhere in the restaurant, but the best seat in the house isn't in the house at all. It's outside. Here, on the sweeping alfresco terrace, you can take in the scene of twinkling city lights and towering Saguaro cacti. If you can swing it, the 5-course Chef's Tasting Menu—$69 per person or a little more than $100 with wine pairings—is the way to go. The portions are smaller but still sizeable and it's a perfect way to beat indecisiveness. The pork belly appetizer, roasted with apple marsala on top of sweet polenta and chanterelle mushrooms, and the winter ale–smoked chicken with a butternut squash risotto, were by far the tastiest parts of the meal, and that's saying a lot.

Duck & Decanter, 1651 E. Camelback Rd., Phoenix, AZ 85016; (602) 274-5429; www.duckanddecanter.com; Deli; $$. When Duck & Decanter first opened its doors in 1972, the neighboring GNC and Sports Authority stores were nonexistent. I like to think about those happier, unchained times as I while the day away on the Duck's cozy outdoor patio with a glass of wine and the Banger. It's a sandwich. Gosh. (Well, actually, at the Duck it's called a "Nooner" but that's beside the point.) This tasty hot treat is made with European sausage, Danish ham, brown mustard, and gruyère cheese, and comes on a delightful French roll. Sandwiches are an art form at this Phoenix landmark, which also doubles as a wine bar and specialty grocer. Duck & Decanter has 2 other locations at 3111 N. Central Ave., Phoenix, AZ 85012; (602) 234-3656, and in Downtown Phoenix at 1 N. Central Ave., Phoenix, AZ 85004; (602) 266-6637.

Fry Bread House, 4140 N. 7th Ave., Phoenix, AZ 85013; (602) 351-2345; Native American; $. For reasons I can't even begin to fathom, Fry Bread House is still a largely undiscovered gem, even among some of the most in-the-know folks in Phoenix. In my case, it's a very special occasion restaurant. Not because the prices are unaffordable, but because, if I were to have my way, I would eat fry bread every day of the week and subsequently my personal trainer would probably kill me. And I like being alive. But if you're visiting Phoenix, it would be a cardinal sin not to indulge your sweet—or savory—tooth at Fry Bread House. In short, fry bread is basically flat dough fried in oil, and in Arizona it is a Native American tradition. You can fold it up to have a fluffier version of a taco. Besides the standard fry bread tacos, this little treasure trove also serves homemade stews, traditional burritos (rolled, in flour tortillas), and some of the best tamales in town.

Postino Winecafe, 3939 E. Campbell Ave., Phoenix, AZ 85018; (602) 852-3939; www.postinoswinecafe.com; Wine Bar; $$. While it's not as old as some of the other places on the Phoenix landmarks list, Postino Winecafe makes the cut for being one of the first wine bars in the area to have made wine more accessible to the masses. It didn't exactly bring in a boatload of varietals that weren't available before, but what Postino did was take away the intimidation factor that people used to feel when deciding between a Chilean and New Zealand Sauvignon Blanc. It helped, too, that the menu was so easy to navigate. It's full of small plates, panini, bruschetta, and salads that encourage sharing to maximize your tasting experience. On Mon and Tues after 8 p.m., $20 will get you any house bottle of wine and bruschetta. Choose 4 of your favorites from options like brie and apples with fig spread, smoked salmon with pesto, and white bean with chopped tomato. The classic fresh mozzarella, tomato, and basil is always good, too. There's also a location at 5144 N. Central Ave., Phoenix, AZ 85012; (602) 274-5144, and an East Valley branch is scheduled to open in Gilbert in fall 2011.

Tarbell's, 3213 E. Camelback Rd., Phoenix, AZ 85018; (602) 955-8100; www.tarbells.com; American; $$$. Chef and Owner Mark Tarbell's résumé is pretty stacked. He served as an apprentice to a Michelin-rated chef, taught courses on French wine at the International Wine School in Cambridge, and cooked for the likes of the Dalai Lama, Muhammad Ali, and Clint Eastwood. He's been a featured chef at the James Beard House in New York seven times, took home the title on Food Network's *Iron Chef America*, served as a panelist at a number of Aspen Food and Wine Classics and, well, you get the drift. The man has skills. His namesake restaurant is elegant but still friendly and relaxed, and is one of those places people come to Phoenix specifically to try. The tuna tartare's cucumber caper vinaigrette makes it one of the best appetizers on the menu, and local produce is the silver bullet in the Tarbell's salad selection, but the one item that takes it all, in my humble opinion, is the house-made pasta Bolognese. It's a simple dish with oregano and parsley, but the organic Maya's Farm tomatoes take it to a whole other level.

ALL-STAR & CELEBRITY CHEFS: VINCENT GUERITHAULT

Vincent Guerithault is credited as the godfather of French cuisine in Phoenix and was the first to fuse the distinguished cuisine and its techniques with the bounty of the Southwest some 25 years ago. Even today, the James Beard Award–winner's clever dishes draw crowds at **Vincent on Camelback** with Guerithault classics like smoked-salmon quesadilla, duck confit tamales, and lobster chimichanga. Yes, and even a tequila soufflé. Let's not forget that.

Vincent on Camelback, 3930 E. Camelback Rd., Ste. 202, Phoenix, AZ 85018; (602) 224-0225; www.vincentsoncamelback .com; French/Southwestern; $$$. It's not rare to come across a really attentive and polite wait staff in Phoenix, but the service at Vincent on Camelback always seems just a little more "on it" than other places. In fact, I'm convinced that it's the staff that has kept this place open for some 25 years. Well, that and Chef Vincent Guerithault's innovative cuisine that is French at its core but with Southwestern accents that produce an unexpectedly delicious hybrid of tastes. A tamale, for example, is sassed up with duck, Anaheim chile, and raisins, while the chimichanga is actually stuffed with lobster and an avocado salsa. Both are appetizers, and both will blow your mind. Main courses are equally as imaginative. Try the boneless Arizona honey-glazed short ribs or the roasted rack of lamb with thyme, rosemary, garlic, and spicy peppers.

Farm-to-Table

Maya's Farm, 6106 S. 32nd St., Phoenix, AZ 85042; (480) 236-7097; www.mayasfarm.com. Owner Maya Dailey is a New Jersey girl who grew up just outside of New York City and always had an eye for environmental science and food. Taking up farming as a hobby on a Gilbert family farm, she tried her hand at growing flowers and herbs and raising chickens for their fresh eggs. Fifteen years later, the hobby turned into a career move when she began selling her fresh vegetables at area farmers' markets. Chefs all over Arizona began requesting her produce for their menus and Maya's little side gig turned into a full-time job. Today, she leases nearly 7 acres of land at the Farm at South Mountain, where you can come pick your own produce, take a tour of the grounds, or sign up for educational seminars on a variety of topics like nutrition and composting.

Specialty Stores, Markets & Producers

Carmel's Coffee Fresh Bakery & Espresso, 4233 E. Camelback Rd., Phoenix, AZ 85018; (480) 251-8888; www.carmelscoffee.com. Owner Pat Flanigan had always wanted to own a coffee shop, and the effort he put into Carmel's Coffee is obvious. It's a laidback spot where you'll find everything from hipsters to suits and families. They come for the homemade baked goods like the buttery, not-too-sweet chocolate chip cookies (his daughter's recipe), warm brown-butter scones, and fresh muffins made from seasonal fruits. The toasted egg and bacon croissant sandwich became a quick favorite, too. Besides delicious coffee, their drink menu also includes fresh-squeezed juice and tea.

Churn, 5223 N. Central Ave., Phoenix, AZ 85012; (602) 279-8024; www.churnaz.com. From the same company that brought you **Postino Winecafe,** Churn is a new spot that is all about artisan ice cream, pastries, cookies, and coffee. I dig the overall minimalist retro feel; its all-white Carrara marble base is punctuated by bright red doors and wallpapered images of turntables. The ice-cream list is all about the basics, too. Churn sticks to classics like vanilla, chocolate, butter pecan, and marble fudge with only 8 flavors. But the important thing is that they do the basics well. The scoops here are as rich and creamy as they come and the pretzel cone is an added bonus!

Gelato Spot, 3164 E. Camelback Rd., Phoenix, AZ 85016; (602) 957-8040; www.gelatospot.com. I'm happy to jump on board the frozen yogurt party train but not at the expense of letting go of my obsession with the silky, buttery delight that is gelato. Especially not when that silky goodness comes from the Gelato Spot and any one of its 150 varieties. Sure, there's a hearty helping of fruit flavors like kiwi, strawberry, and pineapple sorbet, but if you're going to do gelato, do it right with the hazelnut chocolate dream that is the Roche. If for some ungodly reason you don't want to try the gelato, there's also a separate dessert menu with tiramisu, shakes, and frappes. Gelato Spot has 3 other locations at 7366 E. Shea Blvd., Ste. 102, Phoenix, AZ 85254, (480) 367-9900; 4166 N. Scottsdale Rd., Scottsdale, AZ 85251, (480) 425-8100; and 4010 E. Greenway Pkwy., Phoenix, AZ 85032, (602) 494-4010.

Luci's Healthy Marketplace, 1590 E. Bethany Home Rd., Phoenix, AZ 85014; (602) 773-1339; www.lucishealthymarketplace .com. Luci's Healthy Marketplace sells organic and natural products from local and regional vendors. You'll find meats, seafood, dairy, snacks, wine, beer, and even cosmetics and cleaning products. Owner Lucy Schnitzer chooses most of the products herself, and hand selects all of the produce at local farmers' markets. The marketplace also hosts ongoing cooking demonstrations in its state-of-the-art Viking test kitchen. There's a full menu, too, with sandwiches, wraps, sammies, and soups and salads.

Schreiner's Fine Sausage, 3601 N. 7th St., Phoenix, AZ 85014; (602) 265-2939; www.schreinerssausage.com. Family owned and operated Schreiner's Fine Sausage has occupied the same red and white meat shack since 1955. It is the one and only shop of its kind in town and you'll see a lot of Schreiner's specialties on the menu at different restaurants across town. They sell more than 60 varieties of homemade sausages, as well as myriad homemade lunchmeats, slab bacon, hickory-smoked hams, and more. Traditional family recipes were brought over from Germany but there are also influences from Portugal, Spain, England, Poland, and Mexico. Low-fat chicken and turkey products are available for the more health-conscious in bold flavors like the Southwest, a blend of tequila, salsa, and lime juice.

Smeeks Candy Shop, 14 W. Camelback Rd., Phoenix, AZ 85013; (602) 279-0538; www.smeeks.net. The price tags at Smeeks Candy Shop are enough to make you feel giddy, with some reading just 5 cents. Smeeks, located on the far west side of a strip mall, sells things beyond your kitschiest imagination. A rainbow of candy, soda pop, cute lunch boxes, and party hats make it a more innocent, less creepy, version of Willy Wonka. There's even, and this is no joke, an entire section of fake mustaches. Try one, buy it, and enjoy some laughs in the working photo booth. I was tempted to grab one of the giant, multi-colored lollipops and start belting "Good Ship Lollipop" from the rafters, but I don't think they let you finish writing travel guide books from prison. Go to Smeeks and let yourself have a good time. Your inner child will thank you.

Tammie Coe + MJ Bread, 4410 N. 40th St., Phoenix, AZ 85018; (602) 840-3644; www.tammiecoecakes.com. Tammie and M. J. Coe are two in a baker's dozen, she a cake and cupcake extraordinaire and he a bread-baking god. Their 2 Phoenix locations sell her ruffled fondant cakes and cutesy (in a good way) gourmet cupcakes in flavors like milk chocolate hazelnut, red velvet, and strawberry shortcake. And the good news is, you can order directly from their website and have the sweets shipped to your house. M. J.'s marble rye and focaccia are two of the most popular sellers, but one taste test and you'll see they're all worth the trip.

Downtown Phoenix

For some time, it seemed like Downtown Phoenix was at a standstill. Sure, there were sports stadiums, museums, and corporate offices, and the occasional restaurants—some of them good—to service the people that these establishments would bring in, but Downtown Phoenix dining was nowhere near what it is today. Calculated construction and expansion since the early- to mid-2000s brought more attention to the area, but in 2008 the addition of a $1.4 billion light rail system, which starts in North Phoenix and runs through downtown before moving into Tempe and Mesa, ushered in an entirely new consumer base that now had direct access to all of the amenities.

Phoenicians have always had a protective big brother sense about our city center. We always hoped it would someday live up to its natural potential and fiercely fought back against allegations that it would never amount to anything more than an attempted

Downtown Phoenix

E. Indian School Rd.

N. 7th Ave.

N. 7th St.

N. 12th St.

N

1

2

W. Osborn Rd.

E. Osborn Rd.

Park Central
Shopping
Center ■

N. Central Ave.

W. Thomas Rd.

E. Thomas Rd.

3

N. 7th Ave.

4

The Arrogant Butcher	20
Cheuvront Restaurant & Wine Bar	5
Cibo	8
Circa 1900	17
Coach and Willie's	24
District American Kitchen & Wine Bar	12
Downtown Phoenix Public Market	9
The Duce	23
Durant's	3
FEZ	2
Gallo Blanco Cafe & Bar	1
Hanny's	16
Kincaid's Fish, Chop & Steakhouse	21
MacAlpine's Soda Fountain	4
Matt's Big Breakfast	7
Mrs. White's Golden Rule Cafe	22
Nobuo at Teeter House	13
Pizzeria Bianco	18
Portland's Restaurant & Wine Bar	6
Province	11
Sens Asian Tapas	10
Thai Elephant	14
Tom's Restaurant & Tavern	15
Vitamin T	19

17

W. McDowell Rd.

Phoenix
Art Museum ■

E. McDowell Rd.

5

10

6

10

E. Roosevelt St.

7

N. 1st Ave.

9   10   Westin
Phoenix
Downtown

Greater Phoenix Convention
& Bureau Visitor
Information Center

8

11

Arizona State University
Downtown Campus

W. Van Buren St.

12

13   E. Van Buren St.

14

17

15

16

18   E. Washington St.

S. 7th Ave.

20   21

19

22   E. Jefferson St.

US
Airways
Center

23   24

S. 7th St.

S. Central Ave.

Grant
Park

Central
Park

0   0.5   1

MILES

revitalization. So to say that we're excited about the activity in Downtown Phoenix would be a severe understatement. Every time a new business opens in the area, we do a little happy dance.

Besides the light rail, other developments that have had a major impact on the neighborhood's scene in recent years are the Arizona State University Downtown Campus, Phoenix Biomedical Campus, and the $600 million Phoenix Convention Center expansion. And of course there's CityScape, a brand new mixed-use hotspot that is already home to popular culinary destinations like the Arrogant Butcher and Oakville Grocery, and will soon add other eateries to the mix, including a craft beer house, creperie, and sushi restaurant.

And while much of the attention is focused on new development, many restaurants in Downtown Phoenix have set up shop in the area long before the words "downtown renaissance" were uttered in a city hall meeting. Durant's, Tom's Tavern, and MacAlpine's Soda Fountain have all been open for more than 50 years, and still in their original locations. Other restaurants, though they haven't been open for quite as long, pay homage to the history of Downtown Phoenix in other ways. There's Hanny's, which is now a favorite restaurant and bar for Phoenix's hipster crowd but was once the city's first department store, and Pizzeria Bianco and Nobuo at Teeter House, which both feed hungry fans from inside historic homes, the latter being an Arizona bungalow built circa 1899.

Home Grown Chains: Cheba Hut

If your strict virtue deters you from entering a restaurant whose logo incorporates marijuana leaves and subs are served in sizes of "nug," "pinner," and "blunt," you're in luck—**Cheba Hut** delivers! Now open in six different states, Cheba Hut (www.chebahut .com) began toasting subs in 1998, using its marijuana mise en scène to target students at Arizona State University with late-night munchies. Cheba Hut serves healthful vegetarian and meat lovers' subs on your choice of a variety of crunchy, toasted breads. Standouts include the Chronic and AK-47, and if you're not ready to kill your food buzz, order some Hemp Brownies for dessert.

Foodie Faves

The Arrogant Butcher, 2 E. Jefferson, Ste. 150, Phoenix, 85004; (602) 324-8502; www.arrogantbutcher.com; American; $$$. The newest restaurant from the Fox Restaurant Concepts family, the Arrogant Butcher is one of the latest spots to open at downtown Phoenix's CityScape development. Happy hour specials, appetizers, and a cheese menu cater to the after-work business crowd, but the Arrogant Butcher is a winner for lunch and dinner, too. Described by its owners as an "urban grill," dishes include Hama Hama oysters, sweet potato tortelli, short rib stew, grilled swordfish, and more. The

Bolognese entree came with a fantastic ricotta dumpling and crusty garlic bread that was perfect for dipping into the rich sauce. Salads and sandwiches stand their own, too. The turkey Sloppy Joe was savory with a tiny kick from grilled poblano and Pepper Jack cheese.

Cheuvront Restaurant & Wine Bar, 1326 N. Central Ave., Phoenix, AZ 85004; (602) 307-0022; www.cheuvronts.com; Wine Bar; $$. Cheuvront Restaurant & Wine Bar is much beloved by Phoenix oenophiles and has been recognized by both *Bon Appétit* and *Wine Spectator* magazines for its extensive wine list. They have an on-site sommelier, Jeff Grenfell, who hand-chose each bottle on the menu and also can help you pair the right wine with your meal. If you love cheese, Cheuvront's will put you in a state of euphoria. We skipped the pâté but fell in love with the ahi tuna lettuce wrap, a dainty buttercup lettuce dressed in a miso aioli. I went for the risotto cakes for my entree, honestly at first because they were paired with Cakebread Cellars Sauvignon Blanc and I am a fiend for the stuff. The risotto cakes were a delicious vegetarian dish, hearty and fresh with sautéed mushrooms and green peas. As a girl who thinks it's not really dessert without chocolate, the Famous Pumpkin Bread Pudding at Cheuvront's was admittedly delicious. The challah bread is bathed in pumpkin egg custard and then topped with caramel, vanilla whipped cream, and cinnamon. It is moist and delicious, and I would order it again and again.

CityScape Phoenix

A new mixed-use development in Downtown Phoenix, **CityScape** aims to be the area's main dining, nightlife, and entertainment district with more than 620,000 square feet of commercial space. The $900 million project is built on a historic point of origin for Phoenix, where the city's zero-zero address line includes Patriot's Square, a dedicated park honoring city founders and state pioneers.

The combination of commercial, retail, residential, and hotel development is right now the focal point of Downtown Phoenix, where the recession put a halt to most other major construction projects. Valley of the Sun residents and business owners are banking on CityScape to be an expansion catalyst.

New tenants are constantly opening at CityScape but some current popular entertainment locales include Lucky Strike, an upscale bowling alley that caters to adults with beer and cocktail specials, and the comedy club Stand Up Live. It is said to be the largest venue of its kind in the country with 600 seats and a state-of-the-art theater system.

Cibo, 603 N. 5th Ave., Phoenix, AZ 85003; (602) 441-2697; www.cibophoenix.com; Italian; $$. Pronounced "CHEE-boh," the restaurant describes itself as an urban wine bar and pizzeria. It's set in a restored 1913 Arizona bungalow with wood floors, exposed brick, and stained-glass paneling. It is a very charming location made even sweeter on our visit with a seat on the outdoor patio that's

Shopping also is a major draw at CityScape with 6 shops currently open to the public, including Urban Outfitters and West of Soho, which is known for selling top brands at more affordable prices. And, in 2012, Kimpton Hotels & Restaurants will open a 250-room Hotel Palomar. The luxury boutique hotel will serve as a CityScape anchor and include an office tower, the hotel, and a retail plaza. It will be the second Kimpton property for Greater Phoenix and Scottsdale.

But CityScape is, for the most part, focused on dining and nightlife. Locals are eagerly awaiting the opening of places like the Breakfast Club and Brewpublic Craft House. For now, they fill up tables at places like the Arrogant Butcher and Vitamin T—the latest from chef and restaurateur Aaron May that specializes in Mexican street food.

Easy access is an advantage of CityScape. It's bordered on 3 sides by the Metro Light Rail system and neighbors include major event venues like the US Airways Center, Chase Field, and the Phoenix Convention Center. Also only a short walk away is Arizona State University's 15,000-student downtown campus.

strung with twinkling lights. Pizzas on the menu are split into 2 categories—Rosse (red sauce) and Bianche (white pizzas, or no sauce). Naturally, we ordered one of each. We selected from the first category the La Noce, because of the fresh walnuts added on top of mozzarella, ricotta, and arugula. From the second, we chose the Genova with mozzarella, basil pesto, roasted potatoes, white onions, and grated Parmigiano. Of the two, I preferred the simpler flavors of the La Noce and especially liked the addition of crunchy walnuts with the soft cheeses.

Circa 1900, 628 E. Adams St., Phoenix, AZ 85004; (602) 256-0223; www.circa1900bistro.com; American; $$. Circa 1900 was named by the *Arizona Republic* as one of the best restaurants in downtown Phoenix for its simple and tasty contemporary California cuisine. Located in a historic home at Heritage Square, the same spot where you'll find **Nobuo at Teeter House** (see p. 79) and **Pizzeria Bianco** (see p. 81), Circa 1900 Chef Chris Curtiss uses top-quality ingredients in salads like the beet with avocado and pink grapefruit, and main courses that include everything from crispy skate wing to creamy vegetable risotto and braised pork ribs. The diver scallops are a prime example of Circa 1900's unfussy but tasty philosophy. They are served with a simple shallot jus and pearl couscous.

District American Kitchen & Wine Bar, 320 N. 3rd St., Phoenix, AZ 85004; (602) 817-5400; www.districtrestaurant.com; Steakhouse; $$. Inside the Sheraton Downtown Phoenix is District American Kitchen & Wine Bar, a swanky spot where Chef Jay Boginske, who sharpened his skills at other popular restaurants like **Le Grande Orange** and **Zinc Bistro**, serves up accessible but interesting dishes like the rib eye steak that is tender and well cooked, with the flavor perked up by a zesty chimichurri sauce. I appreciate the fact that District, which is housed in a chain hotel, makes an effort to source as many of their ingredients as possible from local purveyors. The fresh baguette is from Phoenix-based **Simply Bread** and comes with **Queen Creek Olive Mill** (see p. 199) olive oil for dipping, an irresistible pairing, and the roasted salmon's risotto is made with asparagus and Arizona sweet shrimp. Every meal at District American Kitchen is topped off with complementary cotton candy, a fun touch.

The Duce, 525 S. Central Ave., Phoenix, AZ 85004; (602) 866-3823; www.theducephx.com; American; $$. The Duce is part thrift shop, part restaurant, and part anything else owners Steve and Andi Rosenstein can dream up. The vintage-flaired 1920s-era warehouse getaway in Downtown Phoenix counts among its attractions an old-fashioned soda fountain, pie stand and bakery, coffee bar, and even a gym. (Maybe to combat all of those Dreamsicle floats and organic screwdrivers?) Meals are cooked and served from a silver retro Airstream trailer and include the best of Andi's family recipes, like the baked kugel, whose hearty casserole texture and apple cinnamon flavor I melted over. The Duce's menu is chock full of sliders of the chicken sausage (another family recipe, specially made by a local butcher only for the Duce), meatball, and brisket variety; maple-roasted spare ribs; and apple crisps, s'more cheesecake, and pecan pie for dessert. Cocktails are made with fresh-pressed fruit and, oftentimes, organic liquor. On Wednesday, visit for karaoke and DJ-spun music.

FEZ, 3815 N. Central Ave., Phoenix, AZ 85012; (602) 287-8700; www.fezoncentral.com; Fusion; $$. FEZ is a favorite among Phoenicians because of its light and fresh cuisine that's a combination of American and Mediterranean flavors. For appetizers, the garlicky hummus or chicken phyllo packets are two of the most popular. The latter are crisp baked and filled with spinach, marinated chicken, roasted red peppers, and feta cheese with a red pepper aioli for dipping. A signature dish, the FEZ Burger throws in some Moroccan flair with a spicy honey molasses barbecue sauce, cinnamon pears, feta, and a lemon garlic aioli on a grilled Angus patty. Crispy onions, cilantro, and a ciabatta bun are delicious bonuses.

Gallo Blanco Cafe & Bar, 401 W. Clarendon Ave., Phoenix, AZ 85013; (602) 327-0880; www.galloblanco.com; Mexican; $$. Once I got over the shock of no free chips and salsa at Gallo Blanco Cafe & Bar (call me spoiled), I was able to appreciate the place for what it is: an easy-to-love, easy-to-order really good Mexican street taco joint. The menu is minimal—you could probably eat your way through it in one sitting if you wanted to—but a prime prototype of the old adage, "quality, not quantity." The Elote Callejero, grilled corn-on-the-cob with Cotija cheese and smoked paprika, tastes so authentic that it takes me back to childhood summers spent on the beaches of Rocky Point, Mexico. On the taqueria list is a

Home Grown Chains: Macayo's Mexican Restaurants

Originally opened in downtown Phoenix in 1946 and made famous for their live music and spirited happy hours, **Macayo's Mexican Restaurants** (www.macayo.com) are tasty staples throughout Arizona and Nevada. Macayo's spots are all vibrantly colored Aztec palace structures you can't help but notice, so don't worry about circling the block to find it. If you're looking for a particularly delicious prickly pear margarita or enjoy dining like the political elite, consider adding Macayo's to your list. President Barack Obama and family celebrated his half-sister's birthday at the original Downtown Phoenix location in 2009.

choice of 5 tacos ranging in price from $2 to $3 each, with the fish option price based on market value. My favorite is the Cochinita, slow-braised pork marinated in achiote spices and garlic. It has a slight citrus tang from the orange zest and guajillo peppers, a small and mild Mexican chile known for its raspberry notes. But the charred tomato salsa on the Carne Asada taco makes it an honorable runner-up, and equally good is the fish taco with a homemade *pico de gallo*. The other 2 options on the list are a vegetarian with seasonal vegetables, *pico de gallo,* and guacamole, and shrimp with chile de arbol, cabbage, and guacamole. There are full entrees at Gallo Blanco, too, but the tacos are why you should eat here. See Chef Doug Robson's recipe for **Pollo Asado** on p. 244.

Hanny's, 40 N. 1st St., Phoenix, AZ 85004-2481; (602) 252-2285; www.hannys.net; American; $$. What was once downtown Phoenix's first department store is now a favorite late-night hangout for area residents and event-goers. Hanny's is a bar first and a restaurant second, so the food isn't exactly innovative but it is good and the place is a fun way to cap off the night after a show at US Airways Arena or play at Herberger Theatre. The menu features appetizers, salads, and sandwiches. Noteworthy items include onion strings, pancetta-wrapped shrimp, chopped salad with hard-boiled egg and avocado, and the P.A.T., a pancetta, arugula, and tomato sandwich on a toasted English muffin. If you like cocktails, Hanny's is your place with its mixture of the classic and contemporary. Their Moscow Mule is one of the most popular in town.

Kincaid's Fish, Chop & Steakhouse, 2 S. 3rd St., Phoenix, AZ 85004; (602) 340-0000; www.kincaids.com; Steakhouse; $$. At this traditional seafood and steak chophouse, a long list of salads, soups, and sandwiches accompanies more hearty dishes like pasta and classic protein entrees. Kincaid's Fish, Chop & Steakhouse is a popular spot for Phoenicians who head downtown for concerts, symphony performances, and other special events. It's a wide-open and welcoming space that is traditional without being too masculine (as far as steakhouses go). The Chophouse Kobe Meatloaf is a favorite amongst diners for its red-wine mushroom sauce and sweet and sour cabbage combination. Meat cuts include filet, sirloin, and rib eye, and accompanying side dishes are downright addictive, especially the truffle-smoked mushrooms.

Matt's Big Breakfast, 801 N. 1st St., Phoenix, AZ 85004; (602) 254-1074; www.mattsbigbreakfast.com; Breakfast; $. At Matt's Big Breakfast, the focus is on traditional morning favorites like fluffy griddlecakes with real maple syrup, Belgian waffles, and omelets made from free-range eggs. I opted for the cheese omelet and was thrilled to see that the accompanying golden hash browns were cooked just right—crispy on the outside, softer on the inside but, most importantly, cooked throughout. You can order items like country sausage, thick cut bacon, and ham a la carte, and definitely should. The meat is from the Pork Shop in Queen Creek in the East Valley and is so juicy and flavorful, you'll consider ordering some to go.

Nobuo at Teeter House, 622 E. Adams St., Phoenix, AZ; (602) 254-0600; www.nobuofukuda.com; Japanese; $$$. James Beard Award–winning Chef Nobuo Fukuda is an absolute genius, but he won't ever admit it. The modest *izakaya* master opened his restaurant in 2010 in a tiny historic 1800s Arizona bungalow, where much of the original structure is still standing, including the beautiful hardwood floors. Foodies who have been following Greater Phoenix and Scottsdale's dining scene for a few years will remember Nobuo for his work at **Sea Saw** in Scottsdale, which closed its doors in 2009. Thankfully, he has hit his stride again at Nobuo at Teeter House, one of the only restaurants in recent years to receive a

ALL-STAR & CELEBRITY CHEFS: NOBUO FUKUDA

Once upon a time in 1978, in a kingdom that I'd never like to visit, the authors of the first guidebook on Greater Phoenix had to explain the term "sushi" to Phoenicians. Thankfully, our knowledge of Japanese food has grown since then, and that's partly due to **Nobuo Fukuda**'s masterful work. His "modern Japanese tapas" at the now-closed Sea Saw in Scottsdale earned him a James Beard Best-Chef Southwest award and his good work continues at **Nobuo at Teeter House** in Downtown Phoenix. The *izakaya* (Japanese tavern) fare is all about small-plate noshing and his multicourse *omakase* (chef's choice) dinners are so imaginative that they could headline their own art exhibit.

full 5-star rating from local food critic Howard Seftel. One meal at Nobuo, and you'll know why. The restaurant's small plates are meant to encourage sharing and a variety of tastes. Standout cold dishes include the Grapefruit & Hamachi. It is thin, fresh, and delicious with avocado and white truffle ponzu oil. I also loved the Ebi Salad. Made with grilled shrimp and rice noodles, the combination of purple basil, mint, cucumber, and glazed peanuts tastes as beautiful as it looks. Hot dishes get slightly heavier with the panko-fried soft-shell crab sandwich. The homemade focaccia and kanzuri aioli were a hit with my entire group. If you can swing it, put yourself in Fukuda's hands with the $130 *omakase* menu, or "chef's choice." See Chef Fukuda's recipe for **Oven-Steamed Sea Bass with Wild Mushrooms** on page 248.

Pizzeria Bianco, 623 E. Adams St., Phoenix, AZ 85004; (602) 258-8300; www.pizzeriabianco.com; Italian; $$. Even if you've never been to Greater Phoenix, you have probably heard about Chris Bianco and his pizzeria downtown. His European-style pies have been featured on *Oprah*, the *Rachael Ray Show*, and even in *Gotham* magazine, where New York City Food Editor Ed Levine declared it the best pizza in the country. The secret? Well, Bianco wouldn't give it away completely but it probably has something to do with his homemade dough, imported ingredients, and wood-fired grill. The short pizza menu includes delights like the classic Margherita, and the Marinara, a simply delicious cheeseless combo of tomato sauce, oregano, and garlic. The Wiseguy was a more complex showstopper with wood-roasted onions, smoked mozzarella, and fennel sausage. A tip, though: Pizzeria Bianco doesn't take reservations and wait times can be long—up to 4 hours in some cases. Arrive early, put your name on the list, and then enjoy some cocktails and appetizers at the neighboring Bar Bianco.

ALL-STAR & CELEBRITY CHEFS: CHRIS BIANCO

Most people probably recognize the name **Chris Bianco** before they've even visited Arizona. That's because his pizza spot, a little place called **Pizzeria Bianco,** has been featured on the Food Network, *Oprah*, and in *Gourmet, Martha Stewart Living*, and *Vogue*, just to name a few. The James Beard Award winner not only runs shop at his Bianco family of restaurants, but also loaned his talents to help bring the Wigwam Resort back from bankruptcy by acting as chief foodie consultant on the menu for **Litchfield's**, the resort's signature restaurant.

Portland's Restaurant & Wine Bar, 105 W. Portland St., Phoenix, AZ 85003; (602) 795-7480; www.portlandsphoenix.com; American/Wine Bar; $$. Portland's Restaurant & Wine Bar differs from some of its neighboring Downtown Phoenix restaurants because it's decked with an interior design that is more about upscale pomp than downtown funk. Rich mahogany wood, tan walls, and dim lighting make Portland's the type of place you could escape to for some downtime with seriously good food. The menu is peppered with generous portions and includes appetizers, salads, burgers, seafood, steak, and homemade pizza. The Pepe Rosso was my favorite from the last category because of its herbed ricotta cheese and roasted red peppers, but the Schreiner's Sausage pasta gave it some competition. Its zesty marinara packed a flavorful punch and the seasonal vegetables were a delightful crispy texture.

Province, 333 N. Central Ave., Phoenix, AZ 85004; (602) 429-3600; http://phoenix.provincerestaurant.com; Fusion; $$. Province is located inside the Westin Downtown Phoenix Hotel and is American cuisine inspired by South American and Spanish flavors. Executive Chef Randy Zweiban uses locally sourced ingredients and the wine list features organic, biodynamic, and sustainable wines from around the world and Arizona. I instantly fell in love with Province's decor—pink walls, vibrant food kaleidoscope images shot by Chef Zweiban's photographer girlfriend, and multi-colored clipboard menus. The attention to design at Province is impeccable. And, while the pink walls may lead you to believe it's more of a place for ladies who lunch, Province's masculine details like sleek, dark wooden chairs and floors make it a great place for the manliest of men, too. The menu at Province makes it easy to share a sampling of dishes with the entire table, which we did and especially loved the crispy white corn croqueta with a slightly spicy ancho aioli, shrimp and Anson Mills organic grits that were the perfect combination of grain and gooey with Manchego cheese, and the Ten Hour BBQ'd Lamb that is served boneless with roasted eggplant and chorizo.

Sens Asian Tapas, 705 N. 1st St., Phoenix, AZ 85004; (602) 340-9777; www.sensake.com; Asian Tapas/Fusion; $$. Chef and owner Johnny Chu spends 4 hours a day at Phoenix's Asian markets, strategically planning his visits around fresh shipments of fish and produce, like the real wasabi root that he uses to marinate the chicken breast. He also handpicked much of his restaurant's glitzy decorations like the Buddha statue, blue neon bar, and lotus-shaped lamps. And, somehow, he's managed to transfer that same attention to detail and care to his staff that is courteous, efficient, and generally just really excited about life. While Sens might look like a nightclub, the food is the real emphasis here with a long list of pan-Asian tapas that are both creative and palate pleasing. The beef marinated in lemongrass is one of the best we tasted. It comes wrapped in a grape leaf, adding a dimension of flavor and making it easier to eat. The sugarcane pork skewers have a unique taste with pineapple ginger sauce, and we ended up ordering a second round of the Papaya Soba spring rolls, mostly as an excuse to shovel more of the peanut dipping sauce onto our plates. The Spicy Saigon, with cauliflower, tofu, and mushrooms, would have been better without the tofu (I'm not a fan) but the spicy basil sauce was a unique surprise.

Thai Elephant, 20 W. Adams St., Phoenix, AZ 85003; (602) 252-3873; www.thaielephantaz.com; Thai; $. Greater Phoenix and Scottsdale have a borderline obsessive Yelp community who dedicate much of their time to reviewing new and landmark restaurants in the Valley. These people know their stuff and recently named Thai Elephant the best Thai restaurant in the Valley of the Sun. Thai Elephant is the type of place where you'll want to kick back for a few hours due to its ultra soothing ambiance of deep red and gold hues. Food here is a complexity of flavor but also very approachable. I was star-struck by the spongy fried fish cakes and their paired floral sauce with cucumbers. Not too greasy, not too fishy, these were a fantastic start to a meal that also included curried chicken, Siamese basil with beef, and a spicy seafood hot pot of mushroom, Kaffir lime, lemongrass, and basil.

Vitamin T, 1 E. Washington St., Ste. 175, Phoenix, AZ 85004; (602) 688-8168; www.eatmoretacos.com; Mexican; $. Is there anything Chef Aaron May can't do? This man has opened restaurants with All-American fare, breakfast favorites, pub grub, and now, Mexican street food. He's a culinary wizard, I'm sure of it. Vitamin T is my go-to when all I want is a cold beer and easy-to-eat, simply good tacos. (In Arizona, you crave this often.) It's a tiny location that fits less than 20 people with a small outdoor patio allowing a few extra spots, and almost every one of these seats is full on any given day. Served on flour or corn tortillas, May's street tacos are priced at 2 for $5 to $7 and come with your choice of *pibil* (pork shoulder), chicken, spicy beef, or vegetarian fillings.

Coach and Willie's, 412 S. 3rd St., Phoenix, AZ 85004; (602) 254-5272; www.coachandwillies.com; American; $$. Stop by Coach and Willie's on game day (Phoenix Suns or Arizona Diamondbacks) and you can bet that both the spacious indoor dining room and front patio will be packed with fans. A longtime local favorite, Coach and Willie's is a chef-backed bar food menu with amped-up appetizers like loaded cheese fries with bacon and green chiles and Major League meatballs wrapped in pizza dough and mozzarella. The specialty salads here are a sight to see and come with a mound of goods. Order the BBQ chicken or crab Cobb for a lighter experience and don't leave without a taste of the cheesesteak sandwich. It's lean roast beef sautéed with caramelized onions, mushrooms, cherry peppers for spice, and garlic mayo.

Durant's, 2611 N. Central Ave., Phoenix, AZ 85004; (602) 264-5967; www.durantsaz.com; Steakhouse; $$$. Durant's has been on the Downtown Phoenix dining scene for more than 60 years and is a classic steakhouse. We're talking waiters in black vests, dark red booths, little lighting, and old-school decor. It reminds me of the "glory days" that I always hear older relatives talk about, when people used to get really dressed up for dinner. You'll find appetizers like oysters on the half shell and shrimp cocktail, prime cuts of meat, no-fuss seafood like trout with tartar sauce, and can't-miss sides like the go-back-for-it-good crab macaroni and cheese.

Order a martini and enjoy the good ol' days at Durant's, a trip down memory lane worth taking again and again.

MacAlpine's Soda Fountain, 2303 N. 7th St., Phoenix, AZ 85006; (602) 262-5545; http://macalpines1928.com; Soda Shop; $. In Greater Phoenix and Scottsdale, new restaurants can spend thousands of dollars trying to make their establishment look vintage. Not MacAlpine's. The retro vibe at this 1950s-inspired soda fountain is completely authentic—right down to the jukebox and

HOME GROWN CHAINS: FOX RESTAURANT CONCEPTS

Fox Restaurant Concepts (www.foxrc.com) boasts 13 original restaurant concepts at 30 locations throughout Arizona and western America. Always upscale, buzz-stimulating, and chic, each of Fox Restaurant Concepts' ventures engenders a new age dining experience where the waitstaff is gorgeous and creatively ingenious chefs design eccentric menus. Fox Restaurants' striking decor conceptualizes an upscale ambiance inspired by honest, artistic food creations. In Greater Phoenix and Scottsdale, check out **Culinary Dropout** (pp. 101 and 221), **Modern Steak** (pp. 114 and 216), **True Food Kitchen** (p. 52), **Sauce, Arrogant Butcher** (p. 70), and more.

collection of antiques sprinkled throughout the shop. Come here for the "phosphate fizzies" and Italian sodas in flavors like "tiger's blood," a combination of cherry and coconut. There's also a vast selection of desserts like pumpkin cheesecake and a list of different floats. Try the pistachio ice cream and amaretto soda—delicious! The '50s music and waitress uniforms are nice touches, too! To continue the fun, sift through the threads at MacAlpine's neighboring vintage store.

Mrs. White's Golden Rule Cafe, 808 E. Jefferson St., Phoenix, AZ 85034; (602) 262-9256; www.mrswhitesgoldenrulecafe.com; Soul Food; $. Mrs. White's Golden Rule Cafe is the type of place you'll swoon over and your doctor will fear. Chicken, pork chops, greens, mashed potatoes—your T-shirt—they're all smothered in some kind of mouthwatering sauce. Arizona's longest-operated African-American business opened in the early 1960s and has been serving deeply dedicated customers some of the best soul food in the Southwest ever since. Rice with gravy, green beans with potatoes, okra gumbo, and slew of other tempting sides accompany main dishes like Southern fried chicken and pork chops. A fun side note: This casual restaurant operates on the honor system. Instead of being presented with a check at the end of the meal, you just tell the cashier what you ordered.

Tom's Restaurant & Tavern, 2 N. Central Ave., Phoenix, AZ 85004; (602) 257-1688; www.tomstavernphoenix.com; American; $$.

Tom's Tavern isn't the place to go if you're looking for a meal that rivals the celebrity chef–run restaurants of New York City. It's a place to go when you want a true taste of Phoenix history. It's been in the same Copper Square location since 1929 and is a longtime favorite haunt for Arizona politicians—one of those "if these walls could talk" establishments. And while Tom's Tavern isn't exactly cutting-edge, it is consistent and the prices are competitive. We'd heard that it was a power lunch spot for the Arizona State Capitol crowd so we visited on a Wednesday afternoon. And while we didn't spot any regular faces (but the place was packed, so they could have been hiding!), we were satisfied with our choices from the long list of sandwiches. The mustard barbecue sauce on the Carolina pulled chicken sandwich was tangy and sweet, and I asked for a small side to dip my curly fries.

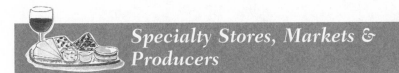

Specialty Stores, Markets & Producers

Downtown Phoenix Public Market, 14 E. Pierce St., Phoenix, AZ 85004; (602) 254-1799; www.foodconnect.org/phxmarket. Downtown Phoenix Public Market is a multidimensional food destination. Here, you'll find **Urban Grocery and Wine Bar** with locally sourced produce, meats, dairy, packaged food items, Arizona wine and beer, and a cafe menu serving breakfast and lunch. There's also the **Royal Coffee Bar** and, on Wednesday and Saturday, an open-air farmers' market. My favorite, though, is Food Truck Friday. It's a weekly event from 11 a.m. to 1 p.m. with trucks from vendors like **Sweet Republic** (see p. 26) ice cream, **Short Leash Hot Dogs** (see p. 25), and **Jamburritos Cajun Grille Express** (see p. 22). Food trucks change on a weekly basis and there's covered seating! (A necessity in the summertime.)

Scottsdale

It's been dubbed "The Beverly Hills of the Southwest," carrying with it a certain expectation of glitz—stylish resorts, serious shopping, and Vegas-style nightlife. I'm happy to report that Scottsdale doesn't disappoint, especially when it comes to the dining scene. Even though it's considered a mid-sized destination, Scottsdale is home to a whopping 600 restaurants. Approximately 100 of these establishments are in the downtown area, a pretty impressive feat considering downtown Scottsdale measures little more than 1 square mile.

But it's here—between Chaparral and Osborn Roads—where you'll find many of the greats: Cowboy Ciao and its ever-popular Stetson Chopped Salad; to-die-for margaritas and pork shoulder tacos at the Mission; and an ever-changing menu with vegetables so good they actually taste like a treat at FnB, a trendy little gastropub that's making big waves in the national media. Downtown is also where you'll find the Old Town Scottsdale Farmers' Market, a weekly Saturday event that not only attracts some of Greater Phoenix's best farmers and purveyors, but also the area's top chefs who have been known to lead cooking classes with produce from the market.

Scottsdale

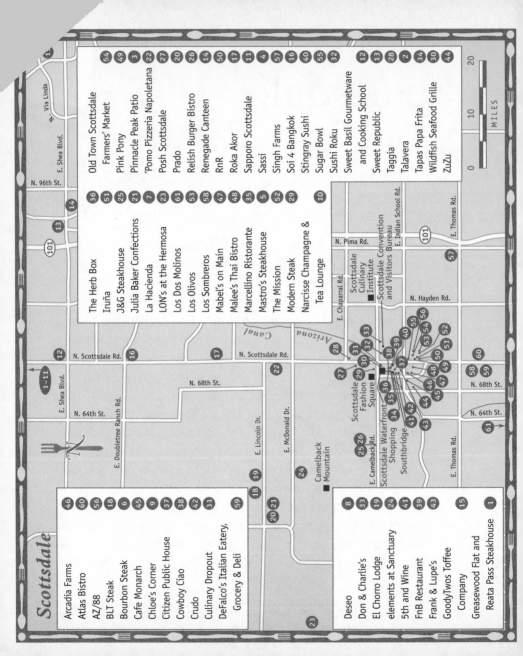

Arcadia Farms — 46
Atlas Bistro — 60
AZ/88 — 56
BLT Steak — 18
Bourbon Steak — 6
Cafe Monarch — 45
Chloe's Corner — 9
Citizen Public House — 37
Cowboy Ciao — 38
Crudo — 42
Culinary Dropout — 31
DeFalco's Italian Eatery, Grocery & Deli — 59

The Herb Box — 36
Iruña — 51
J&G Steakhouse — 25
Julia Baker Confections — 21
La Hacienda — 7
LON's at the Hermosa — 23
Los Dos Molinos — 61
Los Olivos — 53
Los Sombreros — 58
Mabel's on Main — 47
Malee's Thai Bistro — 48
Marcellino Ristorante — 35
Mastro's Steakhouse — 5
The Mission — 52
Modern Steak — 29
Narcisse Champagne & Tea Lounge — 10

Old Town Scottsdale — 54
Farmers' Market — 49
Pink Pony — 3
Pinnacle Peak Patio — 22
'Pomo Pizzeria Napoletana — 27
Posh Scottsdale — 20
Prado — 26
Relish Burger Bistro — 14
Renegade Canteen — 50
RnR — 17
Roka Akor — 11
Sapporo Scottsdale — 4
Sassi — 57
Singh Farms — 16
Soi 4 Bangkok — 40
Stingray Sushi — 55
Sugar Bowl — 32
Sushi Roku — 13
Sweet Basil Gourmetware and Cooking School — 28
Sweet Republic — 2
Taggia — 34
Talavera — 30
Tapas Papa Frita — 44
Wildfish Seafood Grille —

Deseo — 8
Don & Charlie's — 33
El Chorro Lodge — 19
elements at Sanctuary — 24
5th and Wine — 41
FnB Restaurant — 39
Frank & Lupe's — 43
GoodyTwos Toffee Company — 15
Greasewood Flat and Reata Pass Steakhouse — 1

What's also interesting about Scottsdale is that the city is a hotbed for young talented chefs, no doubt because of the two top-rated Le Cordon Bleu culinary campuses that are here. Some of these eager chefs sharpen their skills in area kitchens before moving on to out-of-market opportunities, like *Top Chef* winner Stephanie Izard, but many like Silvana Salcido Esparza of Barrio Cafe and Kevin Binkley of Binkley's in the North Valley stay to brighten the local dining scene.

My introduction to this book mentioned briefly the flurry of celebrity chefs who have been coming out of Arizona in recent years. A lot of these folks come out of this city's restaurants. Before hosting *Worst Cooks in America* on the Food Network, Chef Beau MacMillan of elements at Sanctuary on Camelback Mountain slayed Bobby Flay in a cook-off on *Iron Chef*. Since then, he's cooked for big names like George W. Bush and U2. (Yeah, all of them—even Bono.) Then there's Lee Hilson, executive chef of T. Cook's at the Royal Palms Resort and Spa, who, despite achieving one of the season's highest scores, came up just short in his *Iron Chef* cook-off with Cora. Before you go throwing him a pity party, though, I should mention that Hilson's more than made up for being robbed of the title. T. Cook's made Gayot.com's list of "Top 10 Most Romantic Restaurants in the US" in 2010 and has been voted most popular Scottsdale/Phoenix restaurant by *Zagat's: America's Top Restaurants* twice, in 2006 and 2007.

But there are only so many accolades and titles to go around, right? Regardless of whether they've been recognized by a big shot magazine or foodie organization, there are plenty of restaurants in Scottsdale that are worth your attention. Read up as I break it down!

Foodie Faves

Arcadia Farms, 7014 E. 1st Ave., Scottsdale, AZ 85251; (480) 941-5665; www.arcadiafarmscafe.com; Cafe Fare; $$. I never used to entertain the idea of ordering a salad for an entree until a former coworker introduced me to Arcadia Farms. In my mind, it was a side dish or, at best, a go-to meal when the cabinets, freezer, and refrigerator were void of other options. But then I tried the pesto grilled shrimp salad at Arcadia Farms and a portal to a new world opened itself up to me. I began ordering entree salads at other restaurants because I actually wanted to, not because I felt like I "should." And, while there are plenty of delicious options out there, few compare to those at Arcadia Farms, specifically the one mentioned here. Baby lettuce is topped with a mixture of diced avocado, tomatoes, grilled corn, and goat cheese, and finished with lime vinaigrette. It's pricey at $14 but the portion size is generous and, no matter how I try, I can't replicate the recipe at home so that justifies the cost in my mind. Go back for a second visit to try one of the gourmet sandwiches like the Mediterranean melt, a

combination of roasted seasonal vegetables, smoked mozzarella, and pesto
on ciabatta. Women will love the
decor at Arcadia Farms, too, with its
country bungalow feel and wooden
floors, but men shouldn't let the "ladies
who lunch" atmosphere deter them; the food here is too good.

Atlas Bistro, 2515 N. Scottsdale Rd., Scottsdale, AZ 85257; (480)
990-2433; www.atlasbistrobyob.com; Southwestern, $$$. This BYOB
restaurant is probably one of the most critically acclaimed in the
Valley of the Sun with Southwestern-influenced cuisine that can
include everything from ginger duck breast to applewood-grilled
quail. The "Southwestern" part comes mostly from flavor accents
of things like chili flakes and piquillo pepper, a tiny beak-shaped
pepper known for its distinct sweet and spicy taste combination.
Atlas also is a big supporter of local farms, sourcing from places
like Maya's, McClendon's, and Sphinx Date Farm. Reservations are
definitely recommended, especially between the months of January
and March.

AZ/88, 7353 Scottsdale Mall, Scottsdale, AZ 85251; (480) 994-
5576; www.az88.com; American; $$. This place turns into a bit of a
nightlife hotspot after dinner service so if you aren't a fan of loud
music and crowds, I'd recommend visiting before 9 p.m. But if you
enjoy a little dance action and a kick-ass martini then have at it
until the wee hours of the morning. For lunch and dinner, AZ/88

serves up fancier versions of American classics like hamburgers, sandwiches, and grilled plates in hefty portions. Every time I visit, I vow to order something besides the AZ/88 Chicken Sandwich but I usually just end up alternating between it and the salad version. The spicy buffalo sauce and tangy bleu cheese dressing are just too good to pass up! Split an order of the waffle fries for the table, which come with sides of remoulade, spicy chili ketchup, and Buffalo bleu cheese sauce. If you're looking to go lighter, the Bonfire Chicken plate is a savory option with miniature red potatoes and crisp slaw. AZ/88's minimalist design (white walls, clean lines, and stark black chairs) is punctuated by an ever-changing art installation that I've seen mutate from a Christmas tree of champagne glasses to massive, diamond-crusted greyhound statues, and everything in between.

BLT Steak, 5402 E. Lincoln Dr., Scottsdale, AZ 85253; (480) 905-7979; www.bltscottsdale.com; Steakhouse; $$$. BLT Steak at the Camelback Inn, A JW Resort & Spa was part of the 71-year-old resort's $50 million renovation at a time when Scottsdale was experiencing a high-end steakhouse stampede. A concept from Chef Laurent Tourondel, BLT Steak's weekly specials highlight Southwestern flavors prepared with herbs from Camelback Inn's on-site garden and are easy to spot scrawled across a giant wall blackboard. For the most part, the menu at BLT Steak is all about American steakhouse classics—with the exception of a few dishes where Tourondel's signature French style shines through, like the tuna tartare with avocado and lime dressing—and its chic decor provides a modern backdrop. You'll be hooked the second a note of the restaurant's gruyère popovers wafts past you, but before you crash the dinner party at the next table, know this: Everyone is served these delicious pastry-like bread nuggets. Believe it or not, it only gets better from there: Grilled swordfish in preserved lemon, spice rubbed rib eye, parmesan gnocchi and roasted tomatoes—everything we had on our trip to BLT Steak was better than the last. By the time my chocolate tart rolled around for dessert, I thought I'd died and gone to Tourondel heaven. Its accompanying hazelnut praline ice cream was just over the top.

Bourbon Steak, 7575 E. Princess Dr., Scottsdale, AZ, 85255; (480) 513-6002; www.fairmont.com/scottsdale; Steakhouse; $$$. Michael Mina is a two-time James Beard Award winner who set his sights on the Fairmont Scottsdale Princess in 2008, where he opened Bourbon Steak up to a fan base eager for his award-winning food and contemporary restaurant design. The menu has a section dedicated entirely to Mina classics like the Maine lobster pot pie, a delectable flaky cauldron of vegetables, maitake mushrooms, lobster, and rich truffle cream. The whole-fried chicken for two and grilled Loch Duart salmon are on there, too, in case you were wondering. Steaks like the filet mignon and New York strip are wood-grilled for a wonderful earthy flavor, and sides like truffled mac and cheese and green bean and potato salad make choosing difficult. My recommendation: Go with a group and order a series of sides for the table! Dining at Bourbon Steak can get pricey but the upscale steakhouse has a really approachable happy hour with a $5 bar menu that includes oysters, cheesesteak spring rolls, Bourbon BLT, and more.

Cafe Monarch, 6934 E. 1st Ave., Scottsdale, AZ 85251; (480) 970-7682; American; $$$. Cafe Monarch is the restaurant version of a theatrical monologue; meaning, it's a one-man show. Specifically meaning that the guy who cooks your food (Chris) will be the one to take your reservation (they're required), field your order, and bus your table after you leave. So, needless to say, Cafe Monarch is not the ideal spot if you're looking for a quick bite. But if you want a unique, "Phoenix foodie must-do-before-you-die" experience, then you'll make an appointment to see Chris and his talent at work. Meals are prepared in the open kitchen that juts directly into the small dining room—the entire spot is only 500 square feet—so it's some serious face time with one of Scottsdale's finest chefs. The best thing about Cafe Monarch and Chris is that you can tell the entire operation is a labor of love. If you're interested, he'll tell you all about the dish and the inspiration behind it. The menu here changes daily but past delights have included chicken with chimi-churri sauce and pork loin with roasted green beans and spaghetti-cut crisp potato strings. It's BYOB and cash only, so come prepared.

Chloe's Corner, 15215 N. Kierland Blvd., Ste. 190, Scottsdale, AZ 85254; (480) 998-0202; www.chloescorneraz.com; Cafe Fare; $.

Chloe's Corner at Kierland Commons, with its trendy diner vibe, order-and-sit counter, and grab-and-go options, is the kind of place you'd expect to find in a New York neighborhood. I was a regular here when I worked at Kierland Commons and came every morning for the 50-cent coffee and sometimes the chorizo and egg burrito, which comes wrapped in a warm spinach tortilla with tomatillo salsa, a tart and slightly sweet green sauce. At lunchtime, Chloe's buzzes with business and leisure folks who crowd the cafe for hand-made sandwiches and salads. The American Grilled Cheese is a show-stopper with cheddar, swiss, and white American cheeses, bacon (I ask for extra crispy), and tomato on white bread. Not exactly the epitome of health but, in my opinion, worth the move one notch down on my belt for the day. And while most veggie sandwiches aren't worth the money, I have no qualms about spending the $6.50 for Chloe's version that comes stacked high with lettuce, tomato, swiss, arti-choke hearts, avocado, and onion on wheat with a mayo-mustard spread. You'll also find a selection of craft beers, wine, snack items, old-school candy, and hand-made goods like brownies and cookies.

Citizen Public House, 7111 E. 5th Avenue, Ste. E, Scottsdale, AZ 85251; (480) 398-4208; http://citizenpublichouse.com; Gastropub; $$. Chef Bernie Kantak is the man behind **Cowboy Ciao**'s famed Stetson Chopped Salad (see p. 132) and is now one part of the

trio behind Citizen Public House, a contemporary version of the traditional pub with craft beers, classic and contemporary cocktails, and above-average "pub grub." It's a beautiful space with a large stainless-steel topped center bar, mahogany furniture, and oversized leather booths. Take a closer look to admire some of the framed photos along Citizen's walls—all antique images of the owners' families—and then get down to business. We visited on a busy night and sidled up to the bar where we ordered cocktails first (priorities, people) and shortly after dug into a meal of bacon fat heirloom popcorn (seriously); pork belly pastrami with rye spaetzle and brussels sprouts; and the Halloumi sandwich, a grilled cheese of sorts with chickpea puree, pickles, tomato, greens, and tahini on a *lepinja* roll. It's a Balkan pita-like flatbread that's best when grilled.

Crudo, 7045 E. 3rd Ave., Scottsdale, AZ 85251; (480) 603-1011; www.crudoaz.com; Fusion; $$$. Crudo is an Italian word for raw and that is this restaurant's specialty: sashimi with an Italian flair, i.e.: less ginger, more basil and vinaigrette. I wasn't sure how these two worlds would mesh at first but I left Crudo feeling sublime. Besides sashimi-style seafood, there's also a menu of warm, fully cooked *piatti* dishes. Like most other restaurants in Greater Phoenix and Scottsdale that deal largely with local farmers, Crudo's menu changes quickly and depends on what is in season. However, they do have a selection of signature dishes that you can get anytime, including a delicious albacore tuna sashimi with truffle oil, apples, and black garlic. On the piatti side, I fell in love with the squid ink risotto. It's mixed with pickled chiles, tuna confit, and roasted tomato. The fingerling potatoes in the mushroom au gratin caught my eye and the dish ended up being a favorite of the night. Prepared with seasonal mushrooms, it's drizzled with truffle oil and mixed with mozzarella and fried egg. A surprisingly delicious treat!

Culinary Dropout, 7135 E. Camelback Rd., Ste. 125, Scottsdale, AZ 85251; (480) 970-1700; www.foxrc.com/culinary_dropout; Gastropub; $$. From the beginning, Culinary Dropout was designed to be sort of a "rule breaker" in Scottsdale dining (no uniforms for this trendy staff). I realize that's basically an oxymoron and, while at times the laidback hipster vibe can seem a bit forced, there's no denying the fact that the "amped-up pub fare" at Culinary Dropout is good. Ordering off the antipasti menu makes me giddy with excitement and I love navigating my way through hard-to-find meats and cheeses like *jamón Ibérco* and creamy Italian dolce gorgonzola. This side of the menu also has an assortment of vegetables, the most memorable being 12-hour roasted tomatoes. From the appetizers, skip the house potato chips and the "famous" onion dip, which I'm convinced is a packet of Hidden Valley Ranch powder and sour cream, and instead opt for the soft pretzels with provolone fondue. The shaved prime rib sandwich is so good that I'd come back again just to satisfy cravings for its onion soup dip, and standout entrees include honey-drizzled fried chicken and sweet corn cannelloni with white asparagus and snap peas.

Deseo, 6902 E. Greenway Pkwy., Scottsdale, AZ 85254; (480) 624-1202; www.kierlandresort.com; Latin; $$$. As this book's all-encompassing expert source on the best places to eat in the Valley of the Sun—and there are a ton, believe me—I realize I'm probably not supposed to say this but I will anyway. Deseo is my favorite restaurant in all of Greater Phoenix and Scottsdale. Hands down, without question, no-doubt-about-it—however you want to say it, this place is amazing and, I think, has the best ceviche in town. The man behind Deseo's design and conceptualization, James Beard Award–winning Chef Douglas Rodriguez, is credited as the Godfather of Nuevo Latino cuisine and he's definitely made me an offer I couldn't refuse. (That's the one and only time I'll do that, I promise). My favorite way to maximize the Deseo experience is to skip the entrees altogether (but that doesn't mean they aren't delicious!) and order a variety of things from the ceviche, *entradas* (appetizers), and *verduras y complementos* (sides). The rainbow ceviche is a spectacular party of citrus flavor and a chopped mixture of ahi tuna, salmon, and yellowtail with white soy, sesame seeds, and pickled jalapeño. It was so good that we asked for an extra serving of bread just to dip into the sauce and protested repeatedly when the helpful staff tried to clear the dish to make room for more

ALL-STAR & CELEBRITY CHEFS: BEAU MACMILLAN

When he's not heading the kitchen at Sanctuary on Camelback Mountain Resort and Spa's **elements** restaurant, you can find **Beau MacMillan** hosting the Food Network's *Worst Cooks in America*. He's cooked at the James Beard House, the Aspen Food & Wine Classic, and also has been featured in *Gourmet* and *Bon Appetít* magazine. Besides being the personal chef to Wayne Gretzky, he's put his skills to work for President George W. Bush, Jacques Pepin, and Michele Roux, Sr. In 2006, MacMillan beat Bobby Flay on *Iron Chef America* in the "Battle of American Kobe Beef."

food. I imagine I acted a bit like a snarling momma bear protecting her cubs at that moment, but I didn't care. I was lapping up the rest of that delicious citrus juice come hell or high water. The shrimp chicharron is another beloved dish and, while simple, Deseo's grilled asparagus is downright scrumptious. The *arroz tostado en cazuela* is a more complex taste experience with jumbo lump crab, asparagus, and corn topped with a sunny-side-up fried egg.

elements at Sanctuary, 5700 E. McDonald Dr., Paradise Valley, AZ 85253; (480) 607-2300; www.sanctuaryoncamelback.com; Fusion; $$$. Before taking the reins at elements at Sanctuary on Camelback Mountain Resort and Spa in 1998, Executive Chef Beau MacMillan worked at prestigious spots like Hotel Bel Air and Shutters on the

Beach in California. Since then, he's brought home a victory on *Iron Chef America*, made five appearances on NBC's *Today Show* and hosted his own Food Network program, *Worst Cooks in America*. And while his booming Boston personality makes for great TV, Beau is best in action at elements where he prepares fresh American cuisine with Asian accents. There's a small selection of tasty sashimi like chilled hamachi with avocado, jalapeño, pickled vegetables, and ginger; small plate appetizers including Dungeness crab and spinach "hot pot" with Chinese sausage, wonton chips, and hijiki, a Japanese seaweed; and salads and entrees ranging from barbecue short ribs "Korean style" with vegetable fried rice to mustard-crusted Colorado rack of lamb prepared with braised seasonal greens. Most of the produce at elements is local and organic, and the seafood and meat are sustainable and hormone-free. Vegans and diners on a gluten-free diet will be happy, too, knowing elements staff can work with them on specific dietary restrictions. There's no denying that the food here is the real showstopper, but the atmosphere isn't all that shabby, either. Floor-to-ceiling windows make elements downright magical for dinner and one of the best places to catch a sunset in Scottsdale.

5th and Wine, 7051 E. 5th Ave. Scottsdale, AZ 85251; (480) 699-8001; www.5thandwine.com; Wine Bar; $$. 5th and Wine turns a sprawling industrialized space into a warm atmosphere with living room–style accents like oversized chairs, couches, and brightly colored paintings of dogs doing funny things. Okay, so I'm not exactly sure how many living rooms across the United States actually have paintings of dogs doing funny things, but I just love the ones showcased at 5th and Wine. There's also a large outdoor patio with twinkly lights strung overhead that is one of the best places to enjoy wine in the springtime. Food at 5th and Wine is uncomplicated but good, centered mostly around bruschetta, sandwiches, and salads and shared plates. I recommend going with a group of people and ordering for the whole table. Recommendations from the "share" section include the crispy french fries, which have hints of parsley, garlic, chili, and Pecorino cheese, and are served with a garlic aioli for dipping; chicken drumettes (chicken wings) flavored hot with jicama sticks on the side to mellow out the spice; and the caprese that comes with a creamy, sinfully good burrata cheese. The hummus bruschetta is a little lackluster in presentation but it's tasty, though I still prefer the prosciutto with mascarpone cheese and fig. Happy hour at 5th and Wine is outstanding with $5 wine by the glass, $4 appetizers, and specials on bruschetta. It goes from 3 to 6 p.m.

FnB Restaurant, 7133 E. Stetson Dr., Scottsdale, AZ 85251; (480) 425-9463; www.fnbrestaurant.com; Gastropub; $$$. Meals at FnB in downtown Scottsdale are composed of fresh, locally sourced ingredients whipped up by Chef Charleen Badman, most recently known for her work at **Rancho Pinot** in Phoenix. FnB is a top spot in my book because there's nothing complicated or snooty about it, even as its star rises—most recently making the list of *Food & Wine*'s "10 Best Restaurant Dishes of 2010" for its braised leeks with mozzarella

and fried egg. Menu items are tweaked regularly but you'll find things like spaghetti squash with Campari tomatoes and harissa, a Tunisian chili paste, and scallops with Spanish Salbitxada sauce on top of jasmine rice. FnB's menu lends itself to sharing so this is another place where I would recommend ordering family style. Smiley front-of-the-house master and owner Pavle Milic is just as much of a draw as Badman and her mad cooking skills, too. He'll help you pair any one of Badman's killer dishes with the perfect bottle of wine. And speaking of wine, FnB has gained statewide—and national—recognition for its support of Arizona wines with an all-local list. The gastropub is designed to be a cozy and casual neighborhood joint where the open kitchen is the main focal point. It's a small (and popular) place open Wed through Sun so I recommend making reservations at least a day in advance. See FnB Restaurant's recipe for **Spicy Grilled Broccoli** on p. 235.

Frank & Lupe's, 4121 N. Marshall Way, Scottsdale, AZ 85251; (480) 990-9844; www.frankandlupes.com; Mexican; $$. Frank and Lupe's is a charming little hacienda tucked amongst the galleries in downtown Scottsdale's arts district with a shaded back patio perfect for sipping on ice-cold Tecate or margaritas. There's something about the warm and crispy tortilla chips at Frank & Lupe's that I love, most likely the thicker-than-usual cut that provides for a deeply satisfying crunch every time you bite into one. Mexican

ALL-STAR & CELEBRITY CHEFS: CHARLEEN BADMAN

Charleen Badman shines at **FnB Restaurant,** a culinary darling in downtown Scottsdale serving honest-to-goodness food. The designer of FnB's food and cocktail menu, Badman bucked tradition when she made the kitchen a focal point. Watching her in action—pots, pans, and all—is part of the fun and so is the cocktail list: mint julep, house margarita, and lillet blanc, all made with natural ingredients. Badman hasn't won a James Beard Award (yet) but *Food & Wine* and *the New York Times* recognized her for a menu that makes eating well an adventure.

comfort food is the center of Frank & Lupe's universe and the *carne adobada* burrito plate is the sun. Pork is marinated in red chili sauce with vinegar and oregano, then wrapped in a warm tortilla blanket before being topped with another pour of red sauce. It's on the spicier end of the spectrum but that's nothing a dollop of sour cream can't fix. It's the only time I obey the childhood golden rule of "clean your plate"—rarely do I leave a morsel of even rice or beans on my plate after a visit to Frank & Lupe's.

The Herb Box, 7134 E. Stetson Dr., Scottsdale, AZ 85251; (480) 998-8355; www.theherbbox.com; Cafe Fare; **$$.** The Herb

Box started as a two-woman catering company and most recently opened its second dine-in location here in downtown Scottsdale at the Southbridge development. It is an open and airy space where the beamed ceilings, white-washed wood paneling, and navy blue accents give the restaurant a Northeastern coastal vibe. Open for breakfast, lunch, and dinner, the Herb Box is one of those rare instances where every meal is as good as the last, but if you're there for breakfast, the red velvet pancakes are worth every one of the three exclamation points used to mark their spot on the menu. Stacked 4 cakes high, they are rich and perfectly moist, topped with a scoop of mascarpone crème and Grand Marnier syrup. There's an assortment of delicious salads, sandwiches, flatbreads, and grilled items for lunch, but I am perfectly content to hang out in the market wraps section, where I usually alternate between the chicken arugula with gorgonzola, candied walnuts, and dried cherries, and turkey-avocado with local greens, pepperoncini, tomato, crispy bacon, and jack cheese. Wraps are served with a side of sweet potato chips that are crunchy and devilishly addicting. (Side note: you can buy them by the bag in the adjoining market.) Dinner removes the wraps and sandwiches, and amps up the grilled section. I don't usually gravitate toward salmon dishes but the piquant and sweet combination of the hot honey roasted salmon with an Indian spiced chickpea side dish had me scraping my plate for every last morsel.

Iruña, 7217 E. 1st St., Scottsdale, AZ 85251; (480) 398-3020; www .irunaaz.com; Spanish Tapas; $$$. For what seemed like an eternity, Greater Phoenix and Scottsdale was suffering from a gaping void of quality tapas restaurants. Iruña from Chef Aaron May (who also runs **Over Easy** and **Mabel's on Main** [see p. 111]) was the first to fill that gap with its rotating selection of 20 Spanish and Basque tapas like *chistorra*, a take on classic Spanish chorizo with baby artichoke; spinach and goat cheese croquetas in a rich romesco sauce; and crispy chicken in sweet and spicy glaze. Also try the trio of Spanish cheeses that comes with roasted baby beets and toasted crostini. At the focal point of Iruña's wood-beamed dining room is a floor-to-ceiling mural of the *Sagrada Família* in Spain.

J&G Steakhouse, 6000 E. Camelback Rd., Scottsdale, AZ 85251; (480) 214-8000; www.jgsteakhousescottsdale.com; Steakhouse; $$$. J&G Steakhouse at the Phoenician in Scottsdale is one in a collection of restaurants from Michelin-rated Chef Jean-Georges Vongerichten. The design is as inspired as the food, draped in a rich palate of purple and gold with floor-to-ceiling windows that are perfect for catching those dramatic Sonoran Desert sunsets. J&G Steakhouse is all about premium cuts of meat and a global seafood selection that's complemented by local ingredients and worldly spices. The raw bar is a favorite among seafood lovers, particularly the all-encompassing shellfish platter that comes with lobster, oysters, clams, and jumbo shrimp and mussels. I would have been happy with a meal of the French onion soup and warm beet salad alone, the latter of which is served up with a creamy yogurt dressing and chiles for spice, but, alas, what kind of friend would I be if I didn't try the glazed short ribs for you? I loved the addition of tender carrots for color and taste variety. Paired with a side of roasted mushrooms and creamed corn, it was the ultimate comfort meal after a long day. J&G Steakhouse offers a 5-course tasting menu for $58 per person and happy hour is packed with $5 small plates like charred corn ravioli and sweet and sour pork belly.

LON's at the Hermosa, 5532 N. Palo Cristi Rd., Paradise Valley, AZ 85253; (602) 955-7878; www.hermosainn.com; Southwestern; $$$. LON's at the Hermosa has a 1-acre organic garden just outside its kitchen that chefs, line cooks, and pantry staff tend to every morning, watering produce beds and harvesting things like arugula, basil, peppermint, and chiles for the day's recipes. This on-site harvesting is supplemented with local produce from around Greater Phoenix and Scottsdale, and specialty meats like lamb out of Sonoma and seafood from sustainable fisheries located mostly along the West Coast. LON's specializes in the age-old cooking techniques of smoking, roasting, and wood-grilling with dishes like roasted *jidori* chicken and braised beef short ribs, which are some of the most tender and flavorful I've ever tasted. The ribs are served with seasonal root vegetables—I scored the jackpot with an assortment of red and yellow beets—in a red wine jus that heightens the flavor in a perfect way. And you can't leave LON's without trying the truffle macaroni and cheese. Make a reservation ahead of time to enjoy dinner on the large patio surrounded by rich, colorful foliage. A wonderfully romantic experience!

Los Sombreros, 2534 N. Scottsdale Rd., Scottsdale, AZ 85257; (480) 994-1799; www.lossombreros.com; Mexican; **$$**. Chef and Owner Azucena Tovar puts the flavor and Spanish Colonial charm of San Miguel de Allende to work at Los Sombreros, where the atmosphere is as enchanting as the satiny *mole poblano* sauce that blankets shredded chicken in the restaurant's signature dish. The real fun at Los Sombreros is choosing between mind-blowing entrees like the *Crepas de Mariscos* and crab enchiladas. The latter is a hearty serving of blue crab with a smoky roasted tomato chipotle sauce and smooth cilantro crème and the prior, a seafood medley of fish, shrimp, and crab in a fluffy crepe. Los Sombreros also has more than a dozen fresh margaritas to choose from, and doing so proves to be a challenge with top shelf tequila like Patron Silver and El Tesoro Blanco.

Mabel's on Main, 7018 E. Main St., Scottsdale, AZ 85251; (480) 889-5580; www.mabelsonmain.com; American; **$$**. Mabel's on Main is first and foremost a bar/lounge but it's listed in this book because the menu here, though minimal, is far superior to average bar food. Like, Rockefeller oysters and bluefin tuna carpaccio superior. The lounge is a throwback to the intricacy and sophistication of the 1920s, when bars were speakeasies and people dressed up for grocery shopping. Studded leather seating, embossed tin ceilings, and dark wood furnishing punctuate the design at Mabel's, where, I heard, a secret room will reveal itself if you pull the right book from the shelf at the entryway. Getting back to the food, I loved the seared scallops with gremolata, chicken "lollipop" with Maytag blue cheese dip, and the filet bites that are served with a kicking horseradish cream.

Marcellino Ristorante, 7114 E. Stetson Dr., Scottsdale, AZ 85251; (480) 990-9500; www.5staritalian.com; Italian; $$$. For reasons I don't understand, Marcellino Ristorante doesn't get a lot of play in the local media but I guess it could be because the food here just speaks for itself. Marcellino Verzino is an international chef who came to Arizona by way of New York City, where the *New York Times* heralded him for his work at Riva Grill. Now, at his own restaurant in downtown Scottsdale, he and wife Sima serve up what's been called "The Best Upscale Italian Food in Greater Phoenix" by the *Phoenix New Times*. The wine list here is definitely one to fawn over but the main event is really the food. If you have the time and budget, opt for the "Chef's 5-Course Tasting Dinner" where you can sample a selection of his more than 200 homemade pasta dishes like the Porcini Fettuccine sautéed with shiitake mushrooms, truffle oil, and chunks of fresh lobster. There's also an antipasti course—

the ahi tuna tartare is diced and tossed in a delicious balsamic and lemon dressing—as well as a meat and fish course. If you visit in the winter months, you can't go wrong with Chef Marcellino's osso bucco, a hearty 16-ounce veal shank in a vegetable with saffron risotto.

The Mission, 3815 N. Brown Ave., Scottsdale, AZ 85251; (480) 636-5005; www.themissionaz.com; Latin; $$$. When you walk into the Mission, the first thing you'll think is "I hope the food is as delicious as the design." It is. Set inside a white adobe structure, the Mission's interior is dark and dramatic with rich brown furniture, low-hanging jeweled chandeliers, and a Himalayan salt block wall, whose luminous orange glow is the main source of light in the evenings. Chef Matt Carter is a local favorite who prepares the Mission's modern Latin cuisine in a traditional *plancha*-style flat-top grill that applies direct, radiant heat onto food over pecan and mesquite wood. You'll find influences from Spain, Mexico, and Central and South America at the Mission, where the pork shoulder tacos have become somewhat of a hot commodity. The entree serves 2 and is a pair of whole meat chunks glazed in pineapple, and served with a simple combination of cilantro and red onions with handmade corn tortillas. Other standouts at the Mission include the *pozole*, a traditional Mexican stew with red chile, smoked pork, hominy, avocado, and lime; scallops from the *plancha* stove with smoked tomato, ham, grilled octopus, *requeson* (cheese similar in taste and texture to ricotta), and hearts of palm; and the white bean puree, a side dish made with Cotija cheese, cumin, arugula, and tomato.

Modern Steak, 7014 E. Camelback Rd., Ste. 1433, Scottsdale, AZ 85251; (480) 423-7000; www.foxrc.com/modern_steak; Steakhouse; $$$. After this, I promise never to gush over a restaurant's restroom before the food again. Pinky swear, actually. But the ones at Modern Steak are just so damn snazzy that it would be a shame not to share details with you. Well, I guess I can really only speak knowledgably about the women's restroom: It's top-to-bottom bubblegum pink with the best in girly touches. From the floral wallpaper to sleek white couches and a stunning hydrangea centerpiece, this is a room fit for a princess. In fact, this flirty design carries on throughout the entire restaurant so most of the clientele tends to skew toward girls' night out crowds and couples on a date. The menu reads like a traditional steakhouse with a raw bar, prime beef, and a la carte sides, but the portions are friendlier and accompaniments are meant for sharing. The chopped salad is crisp and refreshing with Parmesan and Champagne vinaigrette, and filet mignon was a main course stunner with cheesy broccoli and buttermilk onion rings on the side. Don't leave without a taste of the loaded fingerling potatoes. They come topped with barbecue short ribs, broccoli, bacon, sour cream, and cheddar. At lunchtime, not even the manliest of men can resist Modern Steak's to-go window with gussied-up hamburgers and french fries.

Narcisse Champagne & Tea Lounge, 15257 N. Scottsdale Rd., Scottsdale, AZ 85260; (480) 588-2244; www.narcisselounge .com; Champagne Bar & Tea Room; $$. This is another one of those Scottsdale establishments that turns into a nightclub atmosphere after 9 p.m., so if that's not your preferred scene, you should be a little more strategic about timing your visit. Happy hour is a good time as there are half-off specials on all food. Highlights on our trip included a smoked salmon platter with avocado and tomato, candied-beet toast with Crescenza cheese and smoked almonds, and a lip-smacking grilled PBJ "slider" with almond butter and grape preserves. Bonus: Happy hour also means 50 percent off well drinks and $5 glasses of bubbly. It runs from 2 to 7 p.m. Sun through Thurs. Narcisse also is a lot of fun for high tea service and definitely a good spot for a group of girlfriends. For $30 per person, you get unlimited tea, choice of sliders (there's a selection of smoked salmon, cheesesteak, shaved turkey, and more), pastries, and "pleasers," dessert goods like chocolate brownies and crème brûlée, as well as a glass of Campo Viejo Cava Rose or Mumm Napa Cuvee M. Decor at Narcisse is part of the fun, too, with bubble-shaped chandeliers hanging from rafters, floor-to-ceiling bottle displays, and a ladies' room whose pink walls look more like bubble gum than a bottle of bubbly.

'Pomo Pizzeria Napoletana, Borgata 6166 N. Scottsdale Rd., Scottsdale, AZ; (480) 998-1366; http://pomopizzeria.com; Italian; $$. There are a handful of pizza places in Greater Phoenix and Scottsdale that can go head-to-head with top players across the country, but 'Pomo Pizzeria is the only place in the Valley of the Sun where the pies are certified authentic Neapolitan-style pizza

by Verace Pizza Napoletana, a Naples-based trade organization whose job it is to uphold the city's traditional pizza standards. Hey, somebody's gotta do it, right? So what does that mean, exactly? Well, for starters the 4 basic ingredients—flour, olive oil, cheese, and tomatoes—come directly from Italy. Pizzas are ultra-thin, too, measuring about 12 inches in diameter and are basically flash-baked—60 to 90 seconds, tops—in a wood-burning oven at 950 degrees. And if that's not OCD enough, regulations even require that the pizza be dressed in a clockwise direction. Feng Shui a la Italia, perhaps? Results are glorious, though, with a crispy outer crust and chewier center topped with even more deliciousness, like the fresh mozzarella and San Marzano tomatoes on the *Quattro Stagioni*. The pie also has a generous helping of sausage, salami, mushrooms, and olives, and is absolutely packed with flavor.

Posh Scottsdale, 7167 E. Rancho Vista Dr., Scottsdale, AZ 85251; (480) 663-7674; www.poshscottsdale.com; Improvisational; $$$. Posh Scottsdale is a chef-owned restaurant in the downtown area specializing in improvisational cuisine. Here's how it works: First choose the number of courses you want, ranging from 4 to 7 rounds and $50 to $80 per person, or $85 to $140 with wine pairings. Next, browse the list of the evening's available proteins—everything from kangaroo to quail and short ribs—and cross off any items that you don't like. Lastly, answer a few questions about your meat temperature preferences, add any special instructions at the bottom, and voila! You're done. Sit back and enjoy your personalized meal prepared by Chef Joshua Hebert the way it was meant to be enjoyed: slowly, in good company, and with the best possible wine pairings. Past dishes have included halibut cheeks in a Meyer lemon aioli and Kobe beef with pickled ramps, a member of the leek family, in wasabi butter.

Prado, 4949 E. Lincoln Dr., Scottsdale, AZ 85253; (480) 627-3004; www.pradolife.com; Italian; $$$. Offering a selection of small and large plates, Prado's menu showcases Chef de Cuisine Peter DeRuvo's creativity, versatility, and talent in creating memorable Italian cuisine. The signature restaurant of the Montelucia Resort & Spa, Prado's wood-fired dishes are the best of farm-to-table freshness and Mediterranean elegance. Menu features change seasonally but the warm marinated Spanish and Italian olives are a must-try mainstay for starters, as are the spiced and honeyed Marcona almonds and velvety burrata with cherry tomatoes and basil. These bites are light but that's the best way to go because variations of handmade pasta tempt at Prado. The rigatoncini with sweet and spicy Schreiner's lamb sausage was tender and mouthwatering with heirloom legumes, local greens, charred tomatoes, chili, and Pecorino cheese. Fish, meat, and poultry dishes are all part of the main course options and lobster is done particularly well with a wild mushroom risotto and mascarpone cheese.

Relish Burger Bistro, 6000 E. Camelback Rd., Scottsdale, AZ 85251; (480) 423-2530; www.thephoenician.com; Hamburgers; $$. Located at the Phoenician resort, Relish Burger Bistro has a selection of 12 fancier-than-average hamburgers like the signature Western Cowboy Burger. Made with grilled Kobe beef, this Southwestern monster is topped with fried onion rings, bacon, jalapeño, sharp cheddar cheese, and Relish's homemade steak sauce. Obviously, it's not for light grazers! But it's a wickedly delicious treat, especially paired with the tater tots and Tecate Pale Lager. Okay, so I'll admit, I actually paired this mother lode of a burger with the chili cheese tots. You only live once, right? I couldn't resist the idea of the gooey melted nacho cheese on top of those crispy potato clouds and the green onions and sour cream, well, they were just icing on the cake.

Renegade Canteen, 9343 E. Shea Blvd., Scottsdale, AZ 85260; (480) 614-9400; http://renegadecanteen.com; Southwestern; $$. There was a collective weep in Scottsdale when news spread that James Beard Award–winning Chef Robert McGrath had sold his beloved **Roaring Fork** to a larger company. Thankfully, he's back in action with Renegade Canteen doing what he does best: slinging the best of the Southwest. Renegade is a medley of the American West's distinctive flavors with influence from Native American, Hispanic, and cowboy cultures. The menu is arranged in small, medium, large, and fish plates with daily specials like oysters and

All-Star & Celebrity Chefs: Robert McGrath

Robert McGrath wears his culinary accolades as proudly as he does his Stetson cowboy hat, and who wouldn't? Everyone from the James Beard Foundation to *Food & Wine* has recognized him, but the man is known as much for his imaginative Southwestern cuisine as he is for his humble attitude. McGrath's Midas touch has played a hand in several Valley of the Sun restaurants, including **Windows on the Green** at the Phoenician and **Roaring Fork**. Today, he's gone back to his campfire-inspired food at **Renegade Canteen,** where the motto is simple: fresh ingredients, classic technique. Culinary gold.

slow-roasted prime rib listed at the bottom. I was thrilled to see McGrath had brought back his famous Green Chile Pork Stew, which is a must-have especially for first-time McGrath diners. It's the perfect amount of spice and topped with jack cheese and served with soft warm tortillas. I split the stew with my dining date and for our second course, we had a fork fight over the last bite of pan-seared trout. It is served with a potato, bean, and bacon salad and mustard greens.

RnR, 3737 N. Scottsdale Rd., Scottsdale, AZ 85251; (480) 945-3353; www.rnrscottsdale.com; American; **$$.** I have to admit that

RnR was a pleasant surprise for me; I wasn't expecting the food at a place run by a nightlife entertainment company (same folks behind Scottsdale clubs like **Axis/Radius** and **Myst**) to be so good. But I gladly ate my words after just one visit. RnR is a massive spot with 2 stories of indoor and outdoor dining space, and is designed as an all-day food and drink hub. For breakfast, the Southwest biscuit and gravy is an early-morning treat with spicy sausage and roasted green chile gravy on top of moist and flaky buttermilk biscuits. Lunch and dinner all-stars include the Dirty Chips, house-made potato chips smothered in blue cheese, tomato, smoked bacon, buffalo sauce, and sour cream; ahi tacos with citrus spice, fire-roasted *pico de gallo*, and guacamole served on jicama tortillas; and a rib eye sandwich lightly pepper crusted with balsamic glazed onions, crimini mushrooms, horseradish cream, and arugula on a French baguette.

Roka Akor, 7299 N. Scottsdale Rd., Scottsdale, AZ 85253; (480) 306-8800; www.rokaakor.com; Sushi; $$$. With a sister location in Chicago, Roka Akor was voted one of the "Top 10 Sushi Spots in the United States" by *Bon Appetít* magazine. There's a small selection of maki rolls, but Roka Akor is really a sashimi lover's dream with fresh helpings of big eye tuna, yellowtail, sweet shrimp, and more. Because sashimi can get pricey for those of us who have never-ending stomachs (so I've heard), I like to supplement my orders with generous helpings of Roka Akor's tempura. Most of this section is made up of vegetarian options like sweet corn and Japanese eggplant, but the butterfish and prawn are delicious, too. Tempura is served with your choice of tensyu or yuzu shichimi dipping sauces. The latter is a fantastic citrus-spice combination and my preferred pairing with the butterfish, asparagus, and bell pepper. Roka also features a traditional Japanese *robata* grill and there's a great selection of vegetables, seafood, and steaks.

Sapporo Scottsdale, 14344 N. Scottsdale Rd., Scottsdale, AZ 85254; (480) 607-1114; www.sapporoscottsdale.com; Japanese/ Sushi; $$. There are some in the foodie world who frown upon teppanyaki because they find it to be "cheesy" but I'm not one of those people—especially when its teppanyaki at Sapporo, where you have basics like chicken and beef in addition to more unique treats such as calamari steak, scallops, and lobster. Every teppanyaki meal comes with a shrimp starter, mushroom soup, house salad, fried rice, and seasonal vegetables with house-made sorbet for dessert. Sushi here also is a worthwhile experience. Try the Scottsdale roll with crab, spicy scallops, avocado, and *kaiware* or the Fuji, which is tempura spicy yellowtail with garlic, cilantro, and lettuce. If you like sushi rolls, you can't go wrong at Sapporo. It's easy to find because it sits just off Scottsdale Road and is a giant, steel-looking structure with large torches lighting its entrance.

Sassi, 10455 E. Pinnacle Peak Pkwy., Scottsdale, AZ 85255; (480) 502-9095; www.sassi.biz; Italian; $$$. Sassi is a romantic spot ideal for celebrating special occasions like anniversaries or birthdays. The North Scottsdale restaurant mimics a Southern Italian villa and is separated into 5 dining areas designed to reflect each room in a home—kitchen, garden terrace, library, wine cellar, and main dining room. Its setting in the foothills of Pinnacle Peak makes for spectacular Sonoran Desert views, but you should know this also means little to no outdoor lighting, particularly along the main roads leading up to Sassi. But you should be fine if you map out the route beforehand and keep your eyes peeled. Like its architecture, the food at Sassi is all about Italy. Handmade pastas, artisanal cheese and salume, fine meat and seafood, and more than 200 Italian wines—it's all on the menu. From the antipasti menu, we fell head-over-heels for the *Spiedino di Fontina*, which is a simple but spectacular marriage of fontina cheese wrapped in prosciutto with roasted red peppers. And, because sharing is encouraged at Sassi, we were able to sample a handful of first and main courses. The risotto was deliciously rich and creamy with nutty porcini mushrooms, artichokes, Parmigiano Reggiano cheese, and truffle oil. I was drawn to the Georges Bank sea scallops because of

their pairing with orange segments and was floored by the delicate citrus accent from the oranges and tomatoes. The dish's *ceci* (chickpea) beans were a nice balancing act, too. There are few things more wonderfully indulgent than dessert at Sassi. Order a glass of Moscato (only $6!) and enjoy it with the *Cannoli della Casa* with ricotta and mascarpone, Grand Marnier, cinnamon, chocolate, and almonds.

Soi 4 Bangkok, 8787 N. Scottsdale Rd., Ste. 104, Scottsdale, AZ 85253; (480) 778-1999; www.soifour.com; Thai; $$. Soi 4 Bangkok burst onto Scottsdale's dining scene with a flurry of accolades from some of the area's toughest food critics and quickly gained a dedicated following. No doubt it has something to do with the restaurant's unique decor, which relies more on trendy design than the typical understated tourist-board posters and floral wallpaper you usually find at other authentic Thai spots. And that's where we hit Soi 4 Bangkok's major draw: its authentic menu that's at its best with the traditional fragrant soups and salads. Starters here are also a delight, particularly the mustard leaf wraps that are rolled around shrimp and roasted coconut. For the main course, the coconut-braised pork shoulder and the grilled skirt steak with vegetables and peanut sauce were both memorable.

Stingray Sushi, 4302 N. Scottsdale Rd., Scottsdale, AZ 85251; (480) 941-4460; www.stingraysushi.com; Sushi; $$. There's no way around my feelings for Stingray Sushi so I'm just going to say it: This is my top spot for sushi in Greater Phoenix and Scottsdale. What I like best about Stingray is that there are plenty of options for "traditional" rolls and sashimi but Executive Chef Andrew Nam also has a collection of more unique rolls, some with Latin—yes,

Latin—influence. I have actually had dreams about eating the Cabo Blanco roll and woken up with a massive craving for the salmon and spicy crab combo. It is rolled together with avocado and cucumbers and topped with chopped halibut, fresh *pico de gallo*, and creamy *ponzu* sauce. At lunchtime, opt for a seat at the sushi bar for free miso soup and salad with your meal. Happy hour is a great time to visit, too, because you get full-sized rolls at crazy values. California and spicy tuna rolls are $3, shrimp tempura roll is $4, and the crispy spicy tuna, Las Vegas, and dragon rolls are each only $5. There's also a location at 2502 E. Camelback Rd., Ste. 156, Phoenix, AZ 85018; (602) 955-2008.

Sushi Roku, 7277 E. Camelback Rd., Scottsdale, AZ 85251; (480) 970-2121; www.sushiroku.com; Sushi; $$$. Located at the W Scottsdale in downtown, Sushi Roku is a part of the collection of restaurants from the Innovative Dining Group that you'll find in places like Hollywood and Las Vegas. It is a sizeable space with natural accents and wood floors. There's also a large sushi bar in the center of the restaurant surrounded by horseshoe booths that give it a slight nightclub VIP feel after dark. (It can get pretty loud in the evenings, too, so it's a fun spot but not the best if you're looking for low-key or romantic.) Obviously, the sushi and sashimi are major draws here, with super-fresh servings of everything from Spanish mackerel to crab and eel. Of the specialty rolls, Sushi Roku lovers have touted the spicy tuna as the best in town, but I'm partial to the more complex Shima roll. It's pricey at $16 but is a generous (by sushi standards) serving of shrimp-wrapped spicy tuna with cilantro and avocado. While it will be hard to pull yourself away from the sushi menu here, the hot appetizers are worth exploring. They're separated into "garden," "sea," and "farm" categories with selections like spicy Shishito peppers in garlic soy sauce, sautéed spicy shrimp with homemade potato chips, and tender Asian BBQ short ribs.

Taggia, 4925 N. Scottsdale Rd., Scottsdale, AZ 85251; (480) 424-6095; www.taggiascottsdale.com; Italian; $$$. Taggia is located inside Arizona's only Green Seal certified hotel, Kimpton's FireSky Resort & Spa, and carries on the hotel brand's commitment to earth-friendly practices. Chef James Siao uses all organic ingredients and supports local farms whenever possible, creating wholesome and straightforward Italian coastal–inspired dishes. For Earth Day, Taggia planned an entire week's worth of celebrations and I was lucky enough to sample the 4-course prix-fixe menu that was a delight from start to finish. The meal began with a salad of local greens, goat cheese, Windmill Farms tomatoes, and baby beets in a citrus vinaigrette, and continued with a primi course of Schreiner's sweet sausage, ramps (wild leeks), and fluffy house-made potato gnocchi and mushrooms. By the time the main course came around, I wasn't sure I'd be able to make it all the way. Ever the eating champ, I managed to work my way through a wild Alaskan halibut dish without leaving so much as a trace of the flaky white fish and its controne bean, fennel, and tomato accompaniments. You'll find the same type of fresh dishes on Taggia's everyday menu. Taggia's interior decor is warm and welcoming with earthy browns, sandy beiges, and rustic orange hues, but the best seat is on its outdoor patio among FireSky's lush tropical landscape that feels like an exotic private island escape. See Chef Siao's recipe for **Burrata with Caponata** on p. 250.

Talavera, 10600 E. Crescent Moon Dr., Scottsdale, AZ 85262; (480) 513-5085; www.fourseasons.com/scottsdale; Steakhouse; $$$. Set high in the foothills of Pinnacle Peak in north Scottsdale, Talavera is a AAA Four-Diamond restaurant in the Four Seasons Resort Scottsdale at Troon North. Its steakhouse menu focuses on locally and regionally sourced ingredients, emphasizing prime cuts of meat, poultry, and game from boutique purveyors as well as a wide variety of seafood. Executive Chef Mel Mecinas—whom you're likely to see around the restaurant, greeting guests by name—is a 13-year veteran of Four Seasons Hotels & Resorts and was one of seven chefs to create a course for the 90th birthday celebration of renowned culinary personality Julia Child. The best time to visit Talavera is for dinner, arriving a few minutes before sunset so you can catch the shades of purple, orange, and yellow as they melt over the Sonoran Desert landscape. It's like a watercolor painting brought to life, a scheme that translates into the restaurant's dining room decor where the focal point is a glass-framed fire element that melds indoor and outdoor dining areas into one cohesive space. Appetizers at Talavera are broken into "warm" and "chilled" categories with items like foie gras (in a cupcake form with a foie gras buttercream and kumquat chutney!) and crab and ahi tuna ceviche. For the main course, choose from Maine lobster, prime steaks, seafood like swordfish and sustainable prawns, and more. Side dishes are ordered a la carte for the table. I've never had a bad one but some favorites include the mixed mushrooms, cheesy gruyère mashed potatoes, and brussels sprouts with fresh beets. Stick around after dinner for complimentary stargazing sessions on Talavera's outdoor patio.

Tapas Papa Frita, 7114 E. Stetson Dr., Scottsdale, AZ 85251; (480) 699-5004; www.tapaspapafrita.com; Spanish Tapas; $$$. Tapas Papa Frita in downtown Scottsdale is a concept revived by owner Joseph Gutierrez after two cycles in the 1990s. Local dining critic Howard Seftel has called its food the "most ambitiously Spanish" of the Greater Phoenix and Scottsdale collection because of its authentic plates like braised oxtail in wine-paprika sauce and snails glazed with sherry vinegar. The list of 50 or so menu items has a series of more accessible options, too, so Tapas Papa Frita is the type of place that will satisfy a wide spectrum of palates with plates like the crab-stuffed piquillo peppers and crispy artichoke hearts. Obviously, tapas are the main draw here but entree-sized portions of paella are worth exploring, particularly the Catalan specialty *arros negre*, with squid, shrimp, and crab over rice. There's also a selection of seafood stews, fish, and steak. Tapas Papa Frita's red and white archways, Joan Miró–inspired art, and live flamenco entertainment will make you feel like you're smack in the middle of Andalusian Spain. The wide selection of Spanish wines (from Tempranillo to Airén and everything in between) doesn't hurt, either.

Wildfish Seafood Grille, 7135 E. Camelback Rd., Ste. 130, Scottsdale, AZ 85250; (480) 994-4040; www.wildfishseafoodgrille .com; Steakhouse; $$$. Wildfish Seafood Grille is a part of Eddie V's Restaurants, Inc., the same company that owns Roaring Fork. It serves up top-notch seafood and prime cuts of meat in a lighter, more modern version of steakhouse ambiance. Here, you'll find things like oysters shucked to order and Foley seafood prepared to your personal liking. In addition to their regular entrees like broiled swordfish with crab and Louisiana red fish, Wildfish Seafood Grille also has a rotating list of main courses that change seasonally. Side dishes like crab fried rice with scallions and mushrooms and sugar snap peas with portobello mushrooms are delicious alternatives to typical steakhouse fare.

ZuZu, 6850 E. Main St., Scottsdale, AZ 85251, (480) 421-7997; www.cafe-zuzu.com; American; $$. ZuZu is the signature restaurant at downtown Scottsdale's Hotel Valley Ho, the city's first year-round resort that attracted Hollywood's elite crowd in the 1950s and '60s. Valley Ho's resurgence in 2005 kept its original midcentury design and walking into its lobby is what I would imagine stepping onto the set of *I Love Lucy* would be like, except in high definition with

All-Star & Celebrity Chefs: Chuck Wiley

Chuck Wiley has been a chef for more than 30 years, most recently heading up operations for **ZuZu** at Hotel Valley Ho. He's also worked for **Sanctuary on Camelback Mountain** and the Boulders Resort & Golden Door Spa. In 2000, Wiley was inducted into the Scottsdale Hall of Fame as Chef Honoree and was named one of "America's Best Hotel Chefs" by the James Beard Foundation. He's showcased his skills at the James Beard House a total of three times and sits on the advisory board for the Scottsdale Culinary Institute.

sunny pops of turquoise, orange, and red. Playing off Valley Ho's 1950s decor, ZuZu and Executive Chef Chuck Wiley's menu is all about seasonal American comfort food with specialties like beef stroganoff, sweet Dijon glazed salmon, chopped salad, and the restaurant's famous sweet and salty warm Parker House Rolls. A meal at ZuZu is the perfect excuse to treat yourself to the type of food you always want to order but pass up for healthier salads and grilled chicken. Yes, they have that, too, but you would be doing yourself a disservice if you didn't order things like the truffled grilled cheese with fontina, arugula, and roasted tomatoes on sourdough (I go the extra mile and add crispy bacon) or the braised beef short ribs that are as tender as the accompanying grits are creamy. They're served with roasted vegetables so it's not a total indulgence, right? I would sell my soul for a batch of really good french fries and ZuZu has some of the best in town. They're twice cooked and served with a spicy Sriracha aioli for dipping, but the best way to enjoy them—remember my note about letting yourself order the fun stuff?—is smothered in chili and cheese. Don't worry; you can take comfort knowing that Chef Wiley uses the best in local, seasonal, and organic ingredients from area farms like Duncan, Sunizona, and Singh. Even the preserves, sausage, feta, goat cheese, and olive oil come from the Greater Phoenix area. Desserts play on the restaurant's retro motif, too, so expect to see banana splits, hot fudge sundaes, and shakes, malts, and floats. The chocolate cherry float was a crowd pleaser on our visit and comes with chocolate malted cocoa nib ice cream and black cherry soda. A delicious homage to the good ol' days!

Landmarks

Cowboy Ciao, 7133 E. Stetson Dr., Scottsdale, AZ 85251; (480) 946-3111; www.cowboyciao.com; Continental; $$$. Cowboy Ciao has been a staple on the local dining scene since 1997. Its name is a nod to the mishmash of modern American and global fare that

ALL-STAR & CELEBRITY CHEFS: TRACY DEMPSEY

Tracy Dempsey is the mad genius behind **Cowboy Ciao**'s bacon chocolate chip cookies whose creations have graced the menus of several high-profile restaurants in Greater Phoenix and Scottsdale, including **Crudo** (see p. 100). She peddles irresistible treats like potato chip ice cream and pillow-like homemade marshmallows at area farmers' markets and recently signed on with **Udder Delights** (see p. 206) in Gilbert to bake seasonal desserts that fall in line with the ice-cream shop's fresh, local approach.

pairs unlikely ingredients into one delicious marriage of flavor, like the chocolate chip and bacon cookies on its dessert menu. There's also a distinct Southwestern influence on Cowboy Ciao's cuisine; case in point: the Exotic Mushroom Pan Fry (my favorite!) that is "mucho mushrooms"—cremini, button, oyster, lobster, black trumpet, and more—in ancho chile cream with avocado and Cotija cheese, a cow's milk hard cheese originating in Mexico. It covers a stack of double-cooked polenta and is a delicious combination of grainy texture and umami taste. The mushroom pan fry is designated as Cowboy Ciao's signature dish but the Stetson Chopped Salad is what initially brings curious newcomers into the downtown

Scottsdale restaurant. Its been plastered in every periodical from *Food & Wine* to *New York* magazine; people have dedicated entire blogs to it; and not-quite-as-good imitations have popped up all across Arizona. The Stetson Chopped is to salads what Robert Indiana's "LOVE" sculpture is to pop art—an icon. It is served in

6 equal columns of Israeli couscous, chopped arugula, roma tomatoes, smoked salmon or chopped grilled chicken, crumbled asiago, and toasted pepitas, black currants, and sweet dried corn, then mixed tableside by your server with a slightly citrus buttermilk pesto dressing. Other interesting items on Cowboy Ciao's menu include Dungeness crab enchiladas and buffalo carpaccio in honey marmalade. Cowboy Ciao is also known for its 3,200 (and counting) wine selections.

DeFalco's Italian Eatery, Grocery & Deli, 2334 N. Scottsdale Rd., Scottsdale, AZ 85257; (480) 990-8660; www.defalcosdeli.com; Italian Deli; $. You'll feel strangely at home at DeFalco's, if home were an Italian grandmother's kitchen where the smell of fresh baked bread, garlic, and fragrant tomato sauce was the norm. It is a maze of shelves piled high with wine, sauce, pasta, and meats imported directly from Italy so getting to the counter empty-handed to place your lunch order is a mighty test of will—something I have yet to accomplish. The first DeFalco's opened in Toronto, Canada, in the early 1900s after the family immigrated from Abuzzi, Italy, and the Scottsdale location has been around since 1972. It is still owned and operated by John and Dora DeFalco and their son, Geraldo. After snaking your way through the labyrinth of temptation, figuring out what to order from DeFalco's long list of sandwiches, pasta, pizza, calzones, and salads is your next challenge. And let's not forget the soups, sides, desserts, and Italian sodas and espresso—oy! Reaching the last bite of my chicken Parmigiano on crispy baguette is always a bittersweet experience because I never want the melted mozzarella and homemade tomato sauce goodness to end. Of the pizzas, the Centurion will make you swoon with spicy soppressata, roasted red peppers, and Gaeta black olives on a traditional bed of mozzarella, basil, and tomato sauce. Treat yourself to a cannoli before you leave—the traditional style is fantastic but I am a sucker for the chocolate shell version.

Don & Charlie's, 7501 E. Camelback Rd., Scottsdale, AZ 85251; (480) 990-0900; www.donandcharlies.com; Steakhouse; $$$. Don & Charlie's is a name synonymous with spring training in Scottsdale thanks in part to its vast collection of sports memorabilia—742 signed baseballs, 300 autographed bats, and 82 jerseys, to be exact. Owner Don Carson is a bit of a collector and his love for college and professional sports has translated into a museum-worthy exhibit that has now crept up onto the ceiling as space in the 450-seat restaurant becomes more limited. Longtime fans like Tracy Ringolsby, a Major League Baseball reporter since 1976, come back for Don & Charlie's traditional steakhouse bites year after year because the food is "always good and consistent." The menu is a long list of barbecue ribs, prime steaks, sandwiches, seafood, and pasta. The complimentary chopped liver that kicks off every meal is something Don & Charlie's devotees swear by and the side dish list is an uncomplicated sampling of basics like onion strings, au gratin potatoes, and steamed broccoli. On any given night, you'll find Don circulating between tables and chatting with guests, but visit during spring training in March and you're likely to see a mixture of baseball players, team managers, and sports announcers in the restaurant's dim lounge.

El Chorro Lodge, 5550 E. Lincoln Dr., Paradise Valley, AZ 85253; (480) 948-5170; www.elchorrolodge.com; Continental; $$$. This 73-year-old Valley of the Sun classic is oozing with Old Arizona charm. Vibrant Western paintings and vintage photographs decorate the interior of a stark white adobe clay building at the base of both Camelback and Mummy Mountains. At sunset, El Chorro Lodge is a magical place where the oranges, reds, and pinks of a Sonoran Desert setting bring to life a large outdoor patio where Scottsdale's finest sip wine and nosh on fresh selections of seared salmon, Porterhouse pork chops, tomato and burrata salad, and Sante Fe chicken enchiladas. Originally opened in 1937, El Chorro Lodge re-launched in 2009 after a brief hiatus. Locals rejoiced in the fact that new ownership kept the restaurant's signature complimentary sticky buns. They are as irresistible and gooey as ever!

Greasewood Flat and Reata Pass Steakhouse, 27375 N. Alma School Pkwy., Scottsdale, AZ 85250; (480) 585-9430; www.grease woodflat.net; Hamburgers; $. **Greasewood Flat and Reata Pass is a**

bar/steakhouse combination that has been serving no-fuss monster burgers to cowboys, bikers, locals, and tourists for more than 30 years from its 120-year-old bunkhouse in North Scottsdale. (Reata Pass is a steakhouse and Greasewood Flat is a bar, so you have to be at least 21 to enter the Greasewood side.) Seating is entirely outdoors on wooden picnic tables and is first-come, first-served, so stake your claim early because this Old West post fills up quick. On the menu are a selection of half-pound burgers—traditional, cheese, green chili, bacon, and any combination of the former—hot dogs, tamales, nachos, chili, and more. I add grilled onions and jalapeño to my green chili cheeseburger. There's something about that Greasewood burger with an ice-cold beer under an Arizona night sky that just feels right.

La Hacienda, 7575 E. Princess Dr., Scottsdale, AZ 85255, (480) 585-4848; www.fairmont.com/scottsdale; Mexican; $$$. At its core, La Hacienda's food is a modern spin on traditional Mexican—*mole poblano*, crispy corn *sope* cakes, and chile relleno are all on the menu—but don't expect to find heavy, sauce-drenched burritos and enchiladas here. Chef Richard Sandoval blends old school tradition with European cooking techniques and whips up a modern version of the classics with a menu focused on lighter, ingredient-driven food. Start with the *camarone* (shrimp) ceviche in a lip-smacking orange chile habanero drizzle and then split the seafood chile relleno appetizer with the table. The poblano pepper is stuffed with crab, scallops, and shrimp, and topped with black bean puree and Chihuahua cheese. A light arbol sauce and cream drizzle add flavor without overpowering. For the main course, sweet potato and a perky green apple salad were palate-pleasing partners to the pistachio and chile ancho–crusted ahi tuna. For a more savory experience, try the beef short rib enchiladas. They're bathed in a light *entomatada* sauce, a spicier version of tomato, with a dollop of wispy *crema fresca*. *Aye, que rico!* Don't leave La Hacienda without ordering a flaming coffee and cinnamon *churro* for dessert.

Los Dos Molinos, 8684 S. Central Ave., Phoenix, AZ 85042; (602) 243-9113; www.losdosmolinosaz.com; Mexican; $$. When you see the word "chile" on the menu at Los Dos Molinos, you'll want to remember that Chef Victoria and crew use New Mexican chiles, which means the spice is undeniably sharp. Family recipes are prepared by Chef Victoria and her daughters—no assembly line here!—and I have a hard time getting past the list of tamales. They're handmade and delicately rolled in a corn husk that helps pack in the spice and flavor, but house specialties like the green chile plate are worth a second look, too. Shredded beef is marinated in a tangy pool of Hatch Valley green chiles and served with rice, beans, and warm flour tortilla. I love spicy food so Los Dos Molinos' *chimichangas* are some of my favorite in town. They are topped with green or red chile sauce, making them a zestier version of the traditional deep-fried burro. There is a second location at 1010 E. Washington St., Phoenix, AZ 85034, (602) 528-3535; and a third location at 260 S. Alma School Rd., Mesa, AZ 85210, (480) 969-7475.

Los Olivos, 7328 E. 2nd St., Scottsdale, AZ 85251; (480) 946-2256; www.losolivosrestaurants.com; Mexican; $$. What started as a cozy adobe-style restaurant in Old Town Scottsdale has turned into a critically acclaimed eatery with the Corral family's second and third generations behind the wheel. And the food isn't the only family-run operation here; an uncle designed and handcrafted its stunning Spanish chandeliers, cousins greet you at the hostess stand, and an old family friend is responsible for the fresh-made tortillas. The Mexican Flag enchilada is a tasty and patriotic delight: a 3-in-1 dish, it comes with a red sauce–topped beef enchilada and 2 cheese versions, 1 topped with sour cream and the other with green chile peppers. The *machaca* (shredded beef) burro is another must-try classic. The meat is sautéed in mush-rooms and onion for a well-rounded savory flavor. There is a second location at 15544 N. Pima Rd., Scottsdale, AZ 85260; (480) 596-9787.

Malee's Thai Bistro, 7131 E. Main St., Scottsdale, AZ 85251; (480) 947-6042; www.maleesthaibistro.com; Thai; $$. Thai restau-rants are often made—or broken—by the quality of their Tom Ka Gai soup so it's not surprising that Malee's Thai Bistro has been a star on the local dining map since 1987. This velvety hot and sour soup is nearly enchanting with its lemongrass notes in a coconut milk broth. It comes with or without chicken, mushrooms, ginger root, and Kaffir lime leaf for citrus flavor, and is garnished with fresh cilantro and green onion. As with any good Thai restaurant, the chef will prepare it to your preferred spice level. Pad thai at Malee's is above average but I prefer the tropical pineapple noodles and no, not just because they're served in a fresh pineapple boat! The shrimp, mussels, scallops, and minced chicken are always fresh and cooked to perfection, and they are the perfect earthy balance to the honeyed smack of pineapples and sweet coconut curry sauce. There's plenty to choose from on the menu at Malee's, and the hardest part is picking from all of the tasty rice, seafood, noodle, and meat dishes!

Mastro's Steakhouse, 8852 E. Pinnacle Peak Rd., Scottsdale, AZ 85255; (480) 585-9500; www.mastrosrestaurants.com; Steakhouse; $$$. Today, Mastro's Restaurants, LLC is a collection of sophisticated, classic steak and fish houses with locations in four different states. But the company started as a single family-owned restaurant in north Scottsdale in 1999. Mastro's does everything with perfection in mind—from petite filets to New York strip steaks and Chilean sea bass. Even for a girl who likes her steak without a single trace of pink (I know, sue me), the proteins are never overcooked or dry. The real fun at Mastro's comes when choosing your sides. Lobster mashed potatoes are a must and the brussels sprouts with crispy pancetta are so good, even your kids would eat them. The Mastro's Signature Warm Butter Cake is one of few desserts I'll choose over chocolate. A scoop of vanilla ice cream tops the moist, pillow-like treat.

HOME GROWN CHAINS: MASTRO'S RESTAURANTS

The average **Mastro's Restaurants** (www.mastrosrestaurants .com) patron has a sophisticated fine wine palate and, most likely, a black American Express card. Decadent, breezy dining rooms offer a dramatic and elegant meal experience where you are encouraged to fine-tune your refined feast. It's the kind of place where your well-bred waiter can recommend the world's best wine pairing and ounces are adjacent to the main entree meats on the menu, not prices. Food critics in Arizona, Illinois, Nevada, and California applaud Mastro's Restaurants, which first opened in Scottsdale in 1999.

Pink Pony, 3831 N. Scottsdale Rd., Scottsdale, AZ 85251; (480) 945-6697; www.pinkponyrestaurant.com; Steakhouse; $$. Pink Pony opened in 1947 at the corner of Main Street and Scottsdale Road in downtown, when what's now the city's main drag was barely a dirt highway. It closed briefly in 2009 but reopened a couple of years later with a fresh coat of paint on its original Pepto-Bismol pink exterior and a revitalized interior that still reflects the warm old-style steakhouse atmosphere locals loved. New owners and Scottsdale residents Danny Little and Tim Smith kept Pink Pony classics like mesquite grilled steaks, chops, seafood, meatloaf, and pot pie on the menu, too. Sides are ordered a la carte. Choose from macaroni and cheese, baked potato, truffle mashed potatoes, and more.

Pinnacle Peak Patio, 10426 E. Jomax Rd., Scottsdale, AZ 85262; (480) 585-1599; www.pppatio.com; Steakhouse; $$. Don't wear a tie to Pinnacle Peak Patio, or you might find yourself watching in disbelief as a server staples it to the rafters. This Wild West outdoor steakhouse is all about laidback cowboy fun with live country music and dancing under the stars. Its menu is a little lengthier than the similar concept from Greasewood Flat and Reata Pass, with a selection of salads, steaks, and baby back ribs added to the mix. What makes Pinnacle Peak Patio stand out from the rest is the fact that it's also a microbrewery with 6 ales and stouts on the menu, like the Cowgirl Blonde Ale with a light Chardonnay-like flavor. It's perfect for those hot Arizona summers!

Sugar Bowl, 4005 N. Scottsdale Rd., Scottsdale, AZ 85251; (480) 946-0051; www.sugarbowlscottsdale.com; Ice Cream; $. *Family Circus* cartoonist Bill Keane often featured the Sugar Bowl in his comics, and you can see a lot of his original works on the walls at this old-fashioned ice-cream and soda shop. Decor and the menu haven't changed much since opening in 1958, but that's exactly the way Valley residents like it. The same pale pink color of Sugar Bowl's exterior is reflected on the inside with oversized vinyl booths, flushed walls, and menus and napkins. It's like stepping back in time or, for you *Grease* fans, like you're hanging with Danny, Sandy, and the gang at the Frosty Palace. Fresh fruit sherbet, malts, shakes, floats, and ice cream are available in a variety of flavors from classics like vanilla and butter pecan to more unique tastes like Turkish coffee and pineapple mint.

Farm-to-Table

Singh Farms, Loop 101 & E. Thomas Rd., Scottsdale, AZ 85251; (480) 225-7199. The culinary world's somewhat recent obsession with all things local and sustainable has turned Singh Farms from a hidden gem into one of the most well-known farms in Greater Phoenix and Scottsdale. Not exactly "off the beaten path," Singh actually sits behind a wall of mesquite trees on the northeast corner of Thomas Road and the Loop 101, one of the area's busiest freeways. Produce from the 20-acre organic farm fills some of the most prestigious menus around town—Prado at the InterContinental Montelucia Resort & Spa is one of them—and everyone from Whole Foods to the Desert Botanical Garden takes their waste to Singh to have it transformed into organic compost, which owners Lee and Ken sell to the public. Enjoy a picture perfect Saturday at Singh, when the farm opens its gates from 9 a.m. to 1 p.m. to those looking to purchase its all-natural goods.

GoodyTwos Toffee Company, 10953 N. Frank Lloyd Wright Blvd., Ste. 105, Scottsdale, AZ 85259; (480) 575-0737; www.goody twos.com. GoodyTwos Toffee Company is owned by a mother and daughter who have mastered the art of combining luscious, all-natural ingredients with innovative flavors that appeal to your most unspoken cravings. Or at least mine. The Cinfully Hazelicious made me want to do bad things—like order an entire 2-pound box and plow through it in one sitting. It is a jubilant mixture of hazelnuts and hazelnut liqueur, spicy Saigon cinnamon, and creamy milk and dark chocolate that's covered—for good measure—with more chopped hazelnuts. And my holidays are no longer complete without GoodyTwos' Comfort & Joy flavor, a Belgian chocolate base with pure peppermint oil and candy crunch. It's laced in a heavenly white chocolate cream.

Julia Baker Confections, 4949 E. Lincoln Dr., Paradise Valley, AZ 85253; (480) 627-3009; www.juliabakercon fections.com. Le Cordon Bleu Paris-trained chef Julia Baker opened her flagship dessert boutique in the plaza of the InterContinental Montelucia Resort and Spa where she dishes out artisan chocolate bites and homemade truffles alongside specialty Champagne, espresso, and wine. Sample each flavor individually or buy an entire box (or, if you're a hog like me, both). While it was hard to pick just one, the hazelnut truffle was a personal favorite with a toasted hazelnut in the center of silky praline cream. The milk ganache was a close second, though, and the ultra smooth French classic dark ganache was a fantastic indulgence, too. Julia Baker Confections is heaven on earth for a chocoholic like me but the passion fruit and raspberry candies are delicious, too.

Old Town Scottsdale Farmers' Market, 3854 N. Brown Ave., Scottsdale, AZ 85251; (623) 848-1234; www.sotfm.com. The Old Town Scottsdale Farmers' Market is arguably one of the best in all of Greater Phoenix and Scottsdale, partly due to the support it's received from area chefs and restaurants. Local favorite **FnB Restaurant** (see p. 105) is there on a regular basis selling handmade goods from culinary master Charleen Badman, and Beau MacMillan from Sanctuary on Camelback Mountain's **elements** restaurant (see p. 103) has been known to take guests on a shop-and-learn cooking trip through the stands. It's held Oct through Aug and features the best local growers in the Valley—like McClendon and Singh Farms—as well as more than 40 vendors that provide a variety of organic vegetables and fruits, flowers, herbs, coffee, and an assortment of handmade items like pastries, jams, and baked goods. On select days, enjoy a bite from the sustainable food truck and enjoy live entertainment and cooking instruction.

Sweet Republic, 9160 E. Shea Blvd., Scottsdale, AZ 85260; (480) 248-6979; www.sweetrepublic.com. Scottsdale's Sweet Republic was voted a "Top 10 Ice Cream Shop" by *Bon Appetit* magazine, which celebrated the artisan ice-cream store's use of all-natural ingredients like slow-roasted bananas and dairy products from independent Arizona farms. They also make their own sorbets, waffle cones, and toppings, all without artificial flavors and hydrogenated oils or preservatives. Twenty-four flavors make up the ice cream list, including slow-churned peanut butter chip with rich chocolate flakes and the more adventurous honey blue cheese. It is one of their most popular items and a savory combination of blue cheese and Arizona honey. There are also shakes, malts, cakes, and sundaes. The Cookie Mintifesto sundae is heavenly and blends mint chip ice cream with chocolate chip cookie chunks, hot fudge, and whipped cream.

Learn to Cook

Sweet Basil Gourmetware and Cooking School, 10749 N. Scottsdale Rd., Ste. 101, Scottsdale, AZ 85254; (480) 596-5628; www.sweetbasilgourmet.com. At Sweet Basil, you get the best of both worlds—the instructors know how to teach and they're experienced chefs who have worked in top kitchens around town. Classes run from Italian to Asian cuisine, and include lectures and demonstrations on techniques, tools, ingredient selection, menu planning, and—my favorite—presentation. You'll learn how to make sauces and soups, and exactly what the terms sauté, braise, grill, and roast mean. There are also fun themed classes like "A School of Fish" focused on preparing coconut shrimp with spicy apricot dipping sauce, Dijon mustard and pretzel-crusted catfish with rice pilaf, and honey-glazed red snapper with orange marmalade parsnips and pears.

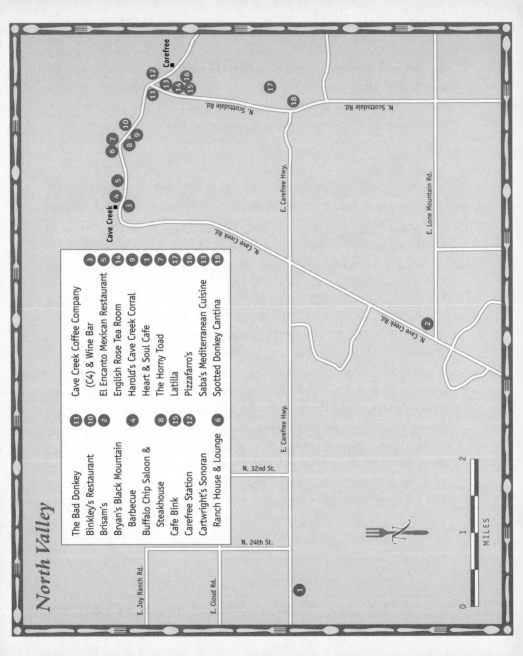

North Valley

The Bad Donkey — 11
Binkley's Restaurant — 10
Brisam's — 2
Bryan's Black Mountain Barbecue — 4
Buffalo Chip Saloon & Steakhouse — 8
Cafe Bink — 15
Carefree Station — 12
Cartwright's Sonoran Ranch House & Lounge — 6

Cave Creek Coffee Company — 11
(C4) & Wine Bar — 3
El Encanto Mexican Restaurant — 5
English Rose Tea Room — 14
Harold's Cave Creek Corral — 9
Heart & Soul Cafe — 1
The Horny Toad — 7
Latilla — 17
Pizzafarro's — 16
Saba's Mediterranean Cuisine — 13
Spotted Donkey Cantina — 18

MILES

N. Joy Ranch Rd.
E. Cloud Rd.
N. 24th St.
N. 32nd St.
E. Carefree Hwy.
Cave Creek
Carefree
N. Cave Creek Rd.
E. Carefree Hwy.
E. Carefree Hwy.
N. Scottsdale Rd.
N. Scottsdale Rd.
E. Lone Mountain Rd.
E. Cave Creek Rd.
N. Cave Creek Rd.

North Valley

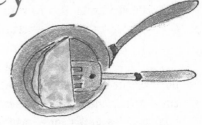

The North Valley is the place to go when you're itching for a dose of Arizona's Western roots. Just past the north Phoenix and Scottsdale areas, you'll find the ruggedly charming towns of Cave Creek and Carefree, where brilliant mountain scenes meander through roads carrying names like Easy Street and Ho Hum Road. There's a noticeably slower pace in the North Valley; it's where residents move to when they're looking for larger plots of land, spacious skies, and more Saguaro cacti than gas stations. It's also a favorite for outdoor enthusiasts who flock to attractions like Bartlett Lake and Spur Cross Conservation Area for hiking, biking, and water sports.

Kevin Binkley is the man often credited for transforming the North Valley's dining scene from kitsch to glitz with his namesake spot, Binkley's Restaurant, which he opened in 2004. He's a Scottsdale Culinary Institute graduate who worked in kitchens across the United States—joining the Inn at Little Washington fresh out of school where he rose to Executive Sous Chef, second in command to Chef and Owner Patrick O'Connell. In 1999, he left "the Inn" for French Laundry, adding a second of the top 13 restaurants in the United States to his résumé. Today, he runs the kitchen and operations at the award-winning Binkley's and big-time critics are taking note: The *New York Times*, *Zagat*, and Gayot.com have all lauded the chef's innovative American cuisine.

Another major culinary destination in the North Valley is Latilla. The AAA Four Diamond restaurant focuses on New American cuisine with flavors inspired by the Southwest—roasted chicken breast with tomatillo salsa, Prince Edward Island mussels in Fresno chili and Dos Equis Lager, and veal sweetbreads with chipotle seasoning. Like Kevin Binkley, the Boulders' Executive Chef Michel Pieton has put in time at top restaurants, except on an international scale. He's sharpened his knives in Michelin-rated French restaurants Le Negre and Restaurant Les Valois Sofitel Hotel, as well as learned from the best stateside masters at US Ritz-Carlton and Four Seasons properties.

Not surprisingly, the North Valley is home to some of the best barbecue in Greater Phoenix and Scottsdale with Bryan's Black Mountain consistently ranking in the top seed. Spotted Donkey Cantina adds a dash of Mexican spice to the lineup. Throw in the English Rose Tea Room and Saba's Mediterranean Cuisine for some Greek nosh and you've got yourself a heaping spoonful of gastronomical goodness worth the trek.

The Bad Donkey, 37636 N. Tom Darlington Dr., Carefree, AZ 85377; (480) 824-1500; www.thebaddonkey.com; Pizza and Subs; $. The Bad Donkey is a grab-n-go (or grab-n-sit) sub and pizza stop with a menu of food that's as fun to read as it is to eat. There are build-your-own options for sandwiches, pizzas, and salads but I chose to put my trust in the Bad Donkey's hands and wasn't disappointed. I have yet to meet a buffalo chicken sandwich that I don't love but the one here is exceptionally good thanks to the added bonus of the restaurant's signature Donkey Sauce, which is basically olive oil with a secret combination of spices. The toasted roll was warm and crisp—just perfect. In a world where veggie pizzas at non-gourmet restaurants are rarely worth their price tags, the Fancy Schmancy Veggie at the Bad Donkey is a pleasant surprise. They call it their "hoitiest, toitiest pie" but I'm willing to put up with the attitude for another taste of its feta cheese and garlic combination with baby spinach and red peppers.

Binkley's Restaurant, 6920 E. Cave Creek Rd., Cave Creek, AZ 85331; (480) 437-1072; www.binkleysrestaurant.com; American; $$$. Binkley's newcomers are often surprised that Chef and Owner Kevin Binkley isn't working in larger markets like New York and San Francisco but, to be honest, he's been there, done that and we're perfectly content having him here in Arizona. For seven years, Chef Binkley has managed to dig deep and come up with an original

All-Star & Celebrity Chefs:
Kevin Binkley

Kevin Binkley's first leap into the restaurant world was as an employee at TCBY where he learned to spin frozen yogurt and make crepes, but foodies should be thankful that his voyage didn't end there. In 2004, he opened **Binkley's Restaurant** in Cave Creek, not exactly a corridor of high-profile restaurants, and still draws people in from every corner of the Valley of the Sun with his daily-changing menu. Binkley has worked with top chefs like Patrick O'Connell (the Inn at Little Washington) and Thomas Keller (French Laundry). He's also a James Beard Award nominee.

6-course menu 5 nights a week, each one more inventive than the last. Past dishes have included octopus with marinated butter beans and spicy green chile; goose egg in an osso bucco ragout; and rib eye beef and barley with brussels sprouts, rutabaga, button mushrooms, and consommé stock. While amuse-bouche at some high-end restaurants are barely more than a bite-sized appetizer, Binkley's are miniature meals of perfection. You'll find things like housesmoked kielbasa with bacon cream and a combination of Spanish chorizo, honey, and gooey mascarpone.

Brisam's, 4730 E. Lone Mountain Rd., Cave Creek, AZ 85331; (480) 595-2202; American; $$. A casual and cozy corner grill/bar/patio, Brisam's is a regular hangout for area residents because of its affordable prices, above average fare, draft beer and wine choices, and super-friendly service. The staff here is the type to remember your name and face, even if you've only visited twice. It's a powder blue interior dotted with chocolate brown booths and fairly large bar, both of which invite you to "stay awhile." While I hesitate to do so because of the negative connotations associated with the term, you could classify Brisam's as having a bar food menu, but only because it has such a varied selection—everything from Philly cheesesteaks (add jalapeño—yum!) to fish tacos and Tuscan chicken pasta with sun-dried tomatoes and artichokes. Because it is a neighborhood hangout, finding seats during lunch and happy hour can be tough, but stick around and make friends—it won't be too hard.

Bryan's Black Mountain Barbecue, 6130 E. Cave Creek Rd., Cave Creek, AZ 85331; (480) 575-7155; www.bryansbarbecue.com; Barbecue; $$. Susie Timm of GirlMeetsFork.com, who I mentioned in the "Keeping Up with Food News" section of this book, is serious about her barbecue. She's part of a professional barbecue team, and has competed and won in several Arizona and Kansas City com-petitions. So when I read her review on Bryan's Black Mountain Barbecue in which she described how the restaurant passed her "sniff test," I had to check it out for myself. Sure enough, the smell of

the pecan wood grill wafted my way before I could step through the door and was so crisp that I could practically taste its smokiness. Inside, Bryan's is quaint and inviting; it's authentic and unpretentious with Western decor and a jazzy neon sign. Taking Susie's recommendation, I sampled the pulled chicken sandwich and wondered how they managed to keep the meat so juicy. The beef brisket and pulled pork were winners, too. My barbecue-fanatic dining partner loved the ribs (pork) but I found them to be a little too chewy. I know they're not supposed to fall off the bone, but I can't help liking them that way! Of the sides, the Six Pack Cowboy Beans stole my heart—they're cooked in beer—and I found the olives in the coleslaw to be a nice salty touch. I'm not surprised that people in all pockets of the Valley of the Sun plan day trips to Cave Creek specifically for Bryan's. See Chef Bryan Dooley's recipe for **Lamb Drumstick with Ginger Beer BBQ Sauce** on p. 242.

Cafe Bink, 36889 N. Tom Darlington Dr., Carefree, AZ 85377; (480) 488-9796; www.cafebink.com; Cafe Fare; $$$. The "little sister" restaurant to Binkley's, Cafe Bink employs many of the same French cooking techniques but in a less-intricate way for a menu that focuses on straightforward, wholesome goodness. The cafe uses local and organic products whenever possible but the menu doesn't change nearly as often as Binkley's. Instead, you'll find standards like the Sloppy Joe—a more dressed-up version of the classic in slider-sized portions with dill pickle and homemade potato chips. There's also a mind-blowing pulled-to-order mozzarella dressed in a red onion marmalade and pesto with confit campari tomatoes; pillow-like gnocchi in a rich butter and Parmesan sauce; bacon-wrapped meatloaf with buttermilk mashed potatoes, cippolini onions and velouté sauce, and much more. No second-child complexes here! Cafe Bink stands tried and true on its own merits and is well worth a visit.

Carefree Station, 7212 Ho Hum Rd., Carefree, AZ 85377; (480) 488-8182; www.carefreestation.com; Fusion; $$. Carefree Station is "a little Southwestern, a little Mexican, and whatever else we like"—or, at least, that's how the owners describe it. Well, they're definitely an accurate bunch. Sushi nachos: a foreign concept in my world before visiting Carefree Station, but I'm oh so glad I had the chance to explore it! You choose from fresh ahi, salmon, or scallops and the nachos come served in 3 different ways—in spicy sesame sauce, poke style, and finally sesame seed-coated and rare, then they're topped with avocado and wasabi aioli. There's also Cowboy Sushi, which is raw or lightly seared beef tenderloin atop crispy potato croquettes, and Fit to Be Thai'd Noodles with straw mushrooms, snow peas, red peppers, asparagus, and cilantro in a light Thai sesame sauce. For those of us missing a cowboy's appetite, Carefree Station offers smaller portions at discounted prices, too.

English Rose Tea Room, 201 Easy St., Ste. 103, Carefree, AZ 85377; (480) 488-4812; www.carefreetea.com; Tea Room; $$. Specializing in the British tradition of afternoon tea, English Rose Tea Room has an extensive menu of authentic food—yes, even beans on toast, the ultimate English comfort food—served with loose leaf teas. You can order salads, quiche, and sandwiches off the lunch menu but the real way to experience the frills and thrills of English Rose is with the Duchess of Bedford's Formal Afternoon Tea option. It is served on a 3-tiered cake stand with the type of fine antique bone china that little girls' dreams are made of. A selection of tea sandwiches makes up the lower tier. Varieties include: chicken with nutmeg and tarragon edged with walnuts, English hothouse cucumber with orange-mint butter, and smoked salmon and cream cheese with lemon. The second tier—a gold mine—has scones dusted in powdered sugar and served with Devon cream. And finally, the grand finale: a selection of seasonal mini cakes, pastries, and petit-fours. Choose from a list of black, green, and herbal teas to round out the experience.

Heart & Soul Cafe, 4705 E. Carefree Hwy., Phoenix, AZ 85331; (480) 595-7300; www.heartandsoulcafeaz.com; Cafe Fare; $$. If you've heard about Heart & Soul Cafe before, and aren't an Arizona resident, it's probably because of the $49, 25-pound Famous Suicide Stack. It is a gluttonous 13 layers of biscuit, chicken fried steak, green pork chili, scrambled eggs with cheese, chicken-fried ham steak, gravy with pinto beans, and even more ingredients that a limited word count won't allow for. I'm not looking to have a heart attack any time soon, so instead I opted for a much more manageable breakfast: the granola raspberry pancakes. They come served with a side of bacon and the 2 cakes were just the right serving size. A sample of the Crazy Biscuits left me with a mild case of food envy. The fluffy biscuit is split in half, one topped with gravy and the other with the restaurant's homemade green pork chili. Two sunny side-up eggs are cracked over the top as a grand finale. Heart & Soul serves lunch, too, with a wide selection of salads and sandwiches like the roast beef and cheddar on 9-grain bread.

Latilla, 34631 N. Tom Darlington Dr., Carefree, AZ 85266; (480) 488-7316; www.theboulders.com; Southwestern; $$$. Once a fine dining destination, Latilla's recent makeover made it more of a casual restaurant—though, you should still reserve your shorts and flip-flops for poolside fun—but the food is still on par with its AAA Four Diamond rating. Executive Chef Michel Pieton's artistry is on display with Latilla's American Southwest menu while the restaurant's romantic white adobe walls exhibit art of a different kind—local and regionally inspired works from New Mexican artist and welder Doug Weigel. We started our adventure with 2 items: organic baby beet salad in blue cheese soufflé and walnut vinaigrette, and Prince Edward Island mussels that bask in a piquant and earthy fusion of chile, roasted garlic, and Dos Equis Lager. Both were equally tasty and beautiful in presentation. For the main course, I chose roasted chicken breast with charred scallions, tomatillo, and a smoked corn salsa. I'll admit part of my reasoning was because the menu told me it only had 404 calories (they highlight the more health-conscious items). You have no idea what a book like this can do to a girl's waistline! I'm happy to report that the roasted chicken was moist, tender, and tasted just as good as—if not better than—my boyfriend's rack of lamb. Latilla also offers a 3-course prix-fixe menu for $39 or $54 with 2 wine pairings.

Pizzafarro's, 36889 N. Tom Darlington Dr., Carefree, AZ 85377; (480) 488-0703; www.pizzafarros.co; Italian; $$. Pizzafarro's is a point of pride for Carefree locals who come back time and again to sample the pies from this family-owned restaurant. The appetizers and salads read like any other restaurant in its genre—chicken wings, garden salad, and garlic bread—so I passed them up to save room for the Pot Luck Special pizza. It was a chewy deep-dish delight with cheese, ground beef, mushrooms, bell pepper, black olives, and onions. With a side order of pepperoncini and cold mug of Stella, it was an affordable and delicious affair.

Saba's Mediterranean Cuisine, 37555 N. Hum Rd., Ste. 109, Carefree, AZ 85377; (480) 575-6574; www.sabascarefree.com; Greek; $$. The strip mall location and photomurals at Saba's Mediterranean Cuisine might not be enough to transport you to Greece, but the food will. So sit back, pop open a bottle of Marathon beer, and let the food whisk your mind away to a sun-drenched Greek island full of tender dolmas, savory spanakopita, and juicy citrus sharwarma chicken. You'll find it all—and then some—at Saba's where the menu might not be inventive but the food is consistent and tasty. I found the Alexandria kebab to be a more manageable alternative to the traditional gyro.

Bite-sized portions of pita bread are topped with thin slices of lamb and covered in a tangy homemade tomato sauce. The salmon kebab was an interesting and light spin with grilled fish, and the tahini on the chicken gyro plate had just the right amount of citrus and cream.

Spotted Donkey Cantina, 34505 N. Scottsdale Rd., Cave Creek, AZ 85262; (480) 488-3358; www.spotteddonkeycantina .com; Southwestern; $$. I was immediately drawn in by Spotted Donkey Cantina's energetic decor. Bright yellow walls are toned down slightly by carved Southwestern-style wood furnishings but the Mexican spirit reaches every corner with ornate crosses and ironwork. It's the perfect backdrop to Spotted Donkey's food. We started with the nachos because the cheddar, manchego, and Monterey Jack seemed like an interesting combination of cheeses and ended up fighting for the last bite. The cheese is melted over a heap of crunchy tortilla rounds, drunken black beans, pulled pork, serrano chile, and roasted tomato and green tomatillo salsa. The beer-braised beef in my enchilada was succulent and packed with flavor, and I loved the kick from its New Mexican hatch and Black Chimayo red chile combo. The "shooters"—tortilla-crusted hand-stuffed cheddar- and bacon-filled jalapeño shots served with creamy cilantro buttermilk—are a must, too. There's also a location at 8220 N. Hayden Rd., Scottsdale, AZ 85258, (480) 922-1400. See Chef Patrick Boll's recipe for **Grilled Corn on the Cob** on p. 238.

Landmarks

Buffalo Chip Saloon & Steakhouse, 6811 E. Cave Creek Rd., Cave Creek, AZ 85331; (480) 488-9118; www.buffalochipsaloon .com; Steakhouse; $$. Buffalo Chip is housed in an Old West frontier-style strip of buildings and is a rockin' time any night of the week with live music, dancing, and—yes—even bull riding competitions. No, I'm not talking about the mechanical kind; that stuff's for suckers (like me). These bulls are alive and kicking—er, bucking—in Buffalo Chip's outdoor pen. If that's a little too wild for your style, there's bound to be a friendly competition of darts happening indoors. Don't come here looking for diet-friendly eats. The words "battered," "fried," and "breaded" are no strangers to Buffalo Chip's menu but isn't that really what you want in a place like this, anyway? Choose from a selection of American goods like burgers, steaks, and skillet meals or go Tex-Mex with tacos, burritos, and enchiladas. I was more than happy with my bratwurst with grilled onions and french fries, and washed it all down with a Bud before making my debut in the bullpen. (Kidding—I wish I was that cool.)

Cartwright's Sonoran Ranch House & Lounge, 6710 E. Cave Creek Rd., Cave Creek, AZ 85331; (480) 488-8031; www.cart wrightssonoranranchhouse.com; Steakhouse; $$$. The interior at Cartwright's was designed to reflect the original ranch house built by Jackson Manford Cartwright, a former Union soldier in the Civil War, in the early 1900s. Old Manny must have had a covered wagon full of cash because this is one snazzy ranch abode. Its exposed beam ceilings, wrought-iron chandeliers, and mesquite wood bar bring to life the more romantic side of the Wild West, and the food is certainly more sophisticated than your average Southwestern steakhouse. I was surprised at how affordable our skillet of steamed clams appetizer was—$6!—and delighted that they didn't sacrifice taste for cost. The ancho chili broth and roasted garlic were savory and delicious with grilled sweet corn confetti on top. It was a chilly night when we visited so I opted for the comfort of beef tenderloin stroganoff as my main dish. The egg noodles were cooked to perfection and the sour cream sauce was rich but not too heavy. There's a selection of steaks and seafood, too. Pick your favorite from the latter category, everything from salmon to ahi and bass, and then decide in which style you want it prepared—Asian, Mediterranean, European, or Sonoran Desert for a mesquite flavor.

El Encanto Mexican Restaurant, 6248 E. Cave Creek Rd., Cave Creek, AZ 85331; (480) 488-1752; www.elencantorestaurants.com; Mexican; $$. El Encanto wins my award for best setting in a Mexican restaurant. It's housed in an Old World mission-style building with a pond at the center. Get a seat on this patio and you could spot ducks, turtles, owls, and even a blue heron. At night, the place lights up with a beautiful orange glow and creates the type of atmosphere that could make even a Taco Bell meal memorable. Not that the food at El Encanto is in any way similar to Taco Bell! In fact, the *Queso Guillermo* still lingers in my mind's palate. It's served so hot that it bubbles over with cheese, yellow chiles, onions, and tomatoes. Add the char-grilled scallions and *machomos* (seasoned crispy beef) to get the full effect. To balance out the appetizer's cheesy goodness, I decided to order the light but flavorful *Camarones de Tequila con Limon*. It's a generous serving of 5 large shrimp that taste like they've been marinating in fresh garlic, cilantro, olive oil, and citrus for days. You'll find *carne asada*, fajitas, enchiladas, and more on the menu, too.

Harold's Cave Creek Corral, 6895 E. Cave Creek Rd., Cave Creek, AZ 85331; (480) 488-1906; www.haroldscorral.com; Italian/Southwestern; $$. Harold's reminds me of a scaled-back version of Cartwright's Sonoran Ranch House & Lounge. It has the same exposed beam ceilings and wood furniture, but instead of wrought-iron chandeliers there are mounted steer skulls, red-and-white-checkered tablecloths, and framed Pittsburgh Steelers jerseys. Harold's has live entertainment, too, but the acts here are slightly larger. Grammy-nominated singer Shawn Mullins was set to play the night after our dinner and David Allen Coe was there a week earlier. And with seating for 800 people, it's no surprise that Harold's moonlights as a concert venue. The food here is a tribute to its Southwestern roots with items like golden brown fried chicken, stuffed hot peppers, and chicken quesadillas, but there's also a selection of steaks and chops and an unexpected Spaghetti Western menu with pasta, pizza, and calzones. I don't really get it but I'm not one to argue with a place that has loaded potato skins and baked lasagna. I'm not sure I'd travel to Harold's all the way from the East Valley (where I live) specifically for the food, but if I were attending a concert there, I'd definitely come early for some of the stuffed peppers.

The Horny Toad, 6738 E. Cave Creek Rd., Cave Creek, AZ 85331; (480) 488-9542; www.thehornytoad.com; Barbecue Steakhouse; $$. The Horny Toad is a family-owned and -operated restaurant that's been serving barbecue, steaks, prime rib, seafood, and burgers for 35 years. Their barbecue has won several awards from local food critics for its mesquite charcoal flavor and tangy homemade sauce. On Monday nights, all-you-can-eat beef ribs bring herds of people out of the woodwork. We ordered a round for the whole table and supplemented the order, which came with coleslaw and fries, with cream cheese jalapeño poppers and sautéed mushrooms. I don't know if it was the twinkling stars, chilly desert night, or the fun of a frontier setting, but something told me that ordering the homemade apple cobbler was good idea—nay, a requirement—and I'm glad I indulged my sweet tooth. The cinnamon swirl ice cream was practically seductive as it melted over the warm, crispy crust. Pure bliss.

Cave Creek Coffee Company (C4) & Wine Bar, 6033 E. Cave Creek Rd., Cave Creek, AZ 85327; (480) 488-0603; www.cavecreek coffee.com. The crowd at Cave Creek Coffee Company (C4) & Wine Bar is an eclectic one with cowboys, city slickers pretending to be cowboys, businesspeople, tourists, hipsters, and stay-at-home moms lining up as early as 6:30 a.m. for their java jolt. C4's coffee is roasted in Cave Creek and their breakfast menu has a reputation that I was hoping it would live up to. Luckily, the Big Ass Burrito is just that: a monstrous tortilla blanket stuffed with eggs, green onion, potato, cheese, salsa, and meat of your choice. I'm a fan of spice so I ordered the chorizo and actually took my leftovers home with me (I live almost 45 miles southeast of Cave Creek) because I couldn't stand the idea of parting with them. Around 5 p.m., the happy hour crowd drifts in for wine, martinis, and light fare like bruschetta and cheese plates.

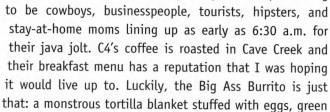

West Valley

Like the rest of Greater Phoenix, the West Valley's origin is rooted in the agricultural industry. First settled in the late 1800s, the area owes its founding to farmers who moved west in search of sunshine and fertile soil, which they found plenty of in the heart of the Salt River Valley. Here, families set up shop and planted seeds that would eventually blossom into promising crops of sugar beets and cotton. These humble beginnings gave rise to a buzzing metropolis that, with approximately 740,000 residents, is one of the largest in all of Greater Phoenix.

The West Valley is actually comprised of 13 different municipalities. The most well known is Glendale. When a railroad link was established in the area in 1895, Glendale grew into the largest town in the area and, when it was finally incorporated in 1910, was still separated from Phoenix by miles of open space. Because of this, Glendale developed separately from the rest of the Valley with its own downtown, banks, grocers, businesses, and neighborhoods. Today, vast stretches of freeway, albeit now dotted with homes and cities along the way, still separate Glendale from the rest of Greater

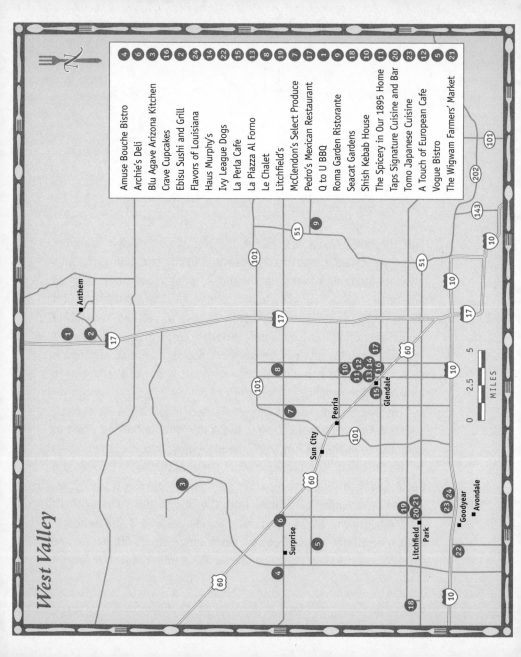

West Valley

N

4 Amuse Bouche Bistro
6 Archie's Deli
3 Blu Agave Arizona Kitchen
16 Crave Cupcakes
2 Ebisu Sushi and Grill
24 Flavors of Louisiana
14 Haus Murphy's
22 Ivy League Dogs
15 La Perla Cafe
13 La Piazza Al Forno
8 Le Chalet
19 Litchfield's
7 McClendon's Select Produce
17 Pedro's Mexican Restaurant
1 Q to U BBQ
9 Roma Garden Ristorante
18 Seacat Gardens
10 Shish Kebab House
11 The Spicery in Our 1895 Home
20 Taps Signature Cuisine and Bar
23 Tomo Japanese Cuisine
12 A Touch of European Cafe
5 Vogue Bistro
21 The Wigwam Farmers' Market

Phoenix's towns. Though, that's not necessarily a bad thing. Its history and development are precisely what gave Glendale the maverick spirit that residents love.

Thanks to the opening of Jobing.com Arena in 2003 and the University of Phoenix Stadium (aka the home of the 2009 NFC Champion Arizona Cardinals) three years later, Glendale has become a hub of sports and entertainment activity in Greater Phoenix, a reputation that was put on display in 2008 when the city hosted Super Bowl XLII. While Glendale's dining scene was definitely respectable before these major events, the planned influx of fans and spectators fast-forwarded preparations for developing additional hotel, recreational, and dining options. Much of Glendale's food adventures are centered around its historic downtown and at Westgate City Center. And, while Glendale and the West Valley don't offer the same caliber of resort and hotel products as, say, Scottsdale, it's a more affordable destination that is well worth its weight in dining gold.

Other major cities in the West Valley include Avondale, Arrowhead, and Peoria, each within 5 to 20 minutes of Glendale by car. The ease of accessibility to the cities means you can drive from one into another without realizing you've crossed any sort of town line. This makes navigating the West Valley a snap. (Just remember, main roads run either south to north or east to west.)

Amuse Bouche Bistro, 17058 W. Bell Rd., Surprise, AZ 85374; (623) 322-8881; www.amusebouche.biz; French; $$. What started as a small catering company grew into one of Surprise's first fine dining establishments in 2008 when husband/wife duo Snir and Kierstin Mor opened Amuse Bouche Bistro in 2008. Since opening, the quaint French bistro has received rave reviews from locals and some of the toughest food critics in town for Executive Chef Matt Ochs's creations. The bone-in braised short rib is a must-try with its green chile polenta and so is the beef tenderloin, a generous thick filet with roasted tomato served on top of melt-in-your-mouth bread pudding. For lunch, you can't go wrong with the quiche Lorraine and soup du jour. Reservations are recommended, though, because the space is small.

Archie's Deli, 17221 N. Litchfield Rd., Surprise, AZ 85374; (623) 546-9967; www.archiesdeli.com; Jewish Deli; $. This New York–style delicatessen is owned and operated by the Wright family, who honed their meat and sandwich shop skills in the Midwest where they were a part of the restaurant business for years. But, when I say New York–style deli, I'm talking strictly about the food and not the ambiance. You won't find the unkempt charm of a Brooklyn shop at Archie's, where the vibe has more of an upscale diner feel. But that doesn't mean the food isn't authentic. Complimentary crunchy dill pickles and extra-garlicky green tomatoes start a meal at Archie's off on the right foot. Follow that up with you-can't-eat-just-one bagel chips with sliced white onion and chopped liver, and you'll be in foodie heaven. Keep it traditional with your sandwich choice and opt for Archie's Reuben, a messy but memorable experience.

Blu Agave Arizona Kitchen, 28615 N. El Mirage Rd., Peoria, AZ 85383; (623) 433-9815; www.bluagaveaz.com; Mexican; $$$. If you do nothing else on your visit to Blu Agave, stake your claim at the bar and order two things: a margarita and an order of the hot home-made tortillas with sweet agave butter. If you find yourself wanting more, and you will, cozy up in one of the oversized banquettes and make a meal out of your visit. The Taco Trio is a great option if you're dining with a group and comes with a medley of 3 different Mexican street tacos: lobster (a personal favorite), *carne asada*, and chicken. If you're wondering what Cabo San Lucas rice is, stop wondering and just order. Its hints of cilantro and lime go perfectly with the New Mexico Style Stacked Green Chili Enchilada. But don't fill up too much on the enchilada because the Lil Churros Mini Doughnuts, irresistible crispy dough sweetened with cinnamon and sugar, are a can't-miss.

Ebisu Sushi and Grill, 39510 Daisy Mountain Dr., Ste. 160, Anthem, AZ 85086; (623) 465-1600; www.ebisurestaurants.com; Japanese; $$. Ebisu is one of seven traditional Japanese gods

HOME GROWN CHAINS: WILDFLOWER BREAD COMPANY

With 12 locations throughout Arizona and homestyle breakfast served until 2 p.m. on the weekends, **Wildflower Bread Company** (www.wildflowerbread.com) has become my go-to lunch destination for a quick, casual bite with friends or when my MacBook Pro and I do brunch (all locations have free wireless). Do yourself a favor and order the roasted sweet potato sandwich. It's served with fresh mozzarella, fig confit, marinated fennel, tomato, and arugula on herb focaccia. Fantastic!

representing, among other things, good luck and health. He's the god of the fisherman and is depicted carrying a large red snapper, which also symbolizes good fortune. So, it makes sense that Ebisu would focus on sushi and fresh Japanese food like blackened salmon salad and miso-marinated sea bass. Try the Bonzai Roll with crab meat, avocado, cucumber, shrimp tempura, and spicy salmon in a sweet eel sauce or the Screaming "O," seared ahi on a bed of daikon drizzled with a spicy pepper sauce. I'm a sucker for noodles, and Ebisu's Yaki Soba was a highlight of the meal. Pan-fried noodles are mixed with sautéed vegetables like celery and bell peppers.

Flavors of Louisiana, 13025 W. Rancho Santa Fe Blvd., Ste. B103, Avondale, AZ 85392; (623) 935-2357; Cajun/Southern; $. If you're looking for tomato-based Creole city Cajun food, look elsewhere because this casual neighborhood spot—owned and operated by a mother and her two daughters—is all about the darker, country Cajun flavors of the bayou. What's the difference? Well, for starters, the jambalaya is more brown than it is the vibrant red color we're all used to seeing in the pretty cookbook photos, and the gumbo is more of a soup texture than stew, but who really cares? It's all delicious and worth ordering. You'll be hard-pressed to find a better po'boy in all of Arizona, too, because Flavors of Louisiana has mastered the secret ingredient: real, quality French bread that is crunchy on the outside, fluffy on the inside. And the flyboys from neighboring Luke Air Force Base who flock to the restaurant for lunch every day? Well, that's just an added bonus.

Ivy League Dogs, 15605 W. Roosevelt St., Goodyear, AZ 85338; (623) 882-2696; American; $. It's not a place where you could spend an afternoon (unless, of course, you really love hot dogs), but that's not really what you would expect from Ivy League Dogs, anyway. Instead, what you should expect is customizable build-your-own dog frenzy where you can pick from toppings like jalapeño, dill pickle, and sauerkraut and add on bacon or fried onions for an extra fee. (Don't pretend you're not curious about what bacon on a hot dog tastes like. The answer is delicious.) The menu comes in a check-sheet format on which you make your selections before handing it to the crew behind the counter. But while the hot dogs are fine and (really) dandy, the real treat for this chocoholic was the deep-fried Oreos.

La Piazza Al Forno, 5803 W. Glendale Ave., Glendale, AZ 85301; (623) 847-3301; www.lapiazzaalforno.com; Italian; $$. Located in downtown Glendale's Historic District, the secret to La Piazza Al Forno is quite literally in the sauce: San Marzano tomatoes imported from Italy, to be exact. The Neapolitan-style pizza (the only true kind of pizza, according to the owners) comes in a variety of flavors but the Mediterranean is a standout, mostly because of the super-fresh and flavorful feta. Antipasti options read like the menu of any other Italian restaurant but the stuffed shrimp, with crabmeat sautéed in a simple olive oil and garlic mixture, are anything but ordinary. I was surprised that the Italian premium beer selection was so affordable at $4.75 and thought the Menabrea Pale was a tasty and not-too-filling complement to the food.

Le Chalet, 5626 W. Bell Rd., Ste. 101, Glendale, AZ 85308; (602) 337-8760; www.lechalet-llc.com; French Swiss; $$. Everything at Le Chalet is a show; from the exhibition kitchen with TV screens that allow you to watch as your crepes are made to the back room where bartenders not only mix your drinks, they keep you entertained with some high-flying bottle antics. But this neighborhood creperie and fondue restaurant doesn't just talk the talk. The Méditerranée crepe is downright stunning, served crispy at the edges and cooked to golden-brown perfection. The sautéed scallops with leeks was an eye-catching combination and it lived up to expectations, especially with the creamy saffron sauce. The La Potence, under "specialty items," is beef tenderloin that is flambéed tableside with whiskey that drips, ever-so-seductively, over a bowl of wild rice. It's a must, especially if you are traveling with a group of people. And, of course, you can't leave Le Chalet without trying the traditional swiss cheese fondue or dessert, for that matter.

Litchfield's, 300 E. Wigwam Blvd., Litchfield Park, AZ 85340; (623) 935-3811; www.wigwamarizona.com; Steakhouse; $$$. The Wigwam Resort, an 82-year-old property that's been a longtime favorite of Phoenix-area locals, faced bankruptcy in 2009 before Jerry Colangelo and partners poured $7 million into renovating the West Valley jewel. With the revamp came the opening of Litchfield's, a dinner-only spot that is all about locally sourced, farm-to-table dishes. On the menu you'll find Arizona trout and grass-fed beef as well as produce from nearby farms like **Queen Creek Olive Mill** (see p. 199). Oh, and did I mention that Litchfield's menu was developed by James Beard Award–winning Chef Chris Bianco? That always helps.

Q to U BBQ, 3434 W. Anthem Way, Ste. 146, Anthem, AZ 85086; (623) 465-7800; www.q-to-u-bbq.com; Barbecue; $$. Owned by the Rosol family, Q to U BBQ specializes in slow-smoked meats.

The family regularly competes in Kansas City Barbecue Society-sanctioned competitions under the team name Toys 4 BBQ'N and in 2008 ranked as the 4th best team in Arizona for competitive barbecue. On the appetizer menu, the smoke-fried wings were crunchy and flavorful but the pulled pork nachos were the hands-down favorite of the night. Q to U is a good option for families or groups because you can order meat like brisket or pulled chicken by the pound. Sample platters are great for sampling a piece of everything.

Roma Garden Ristorante, 3923 E. Thunderbird Rd., Ste. 113, Phoenix, AZ 85032; (602) 788-5466; www.romagarden.com; Italian; $$$. To say that the outside façade of Roma Garden Ristorante is nondescript is a bit of an understatement; it's next door to a Panda Express and just doors down from a water mart. But don't let the location fool you. The food at Roma Garden is anything but ordinary. In fact, there are a handful of diehard local foodies who have called it the most authentic Italian food in Phoenix. Portions are generous, ingredients are fresh, and pasta is al dente—the way it's supposed to be. You'll find everything from braised lamb shank to osso bucco, chicken cacciatore, and veal marsala. Roma Garden is family-owned and -operated, so expect to see Owner Vjeko Marcelic and crew running around serving tables, clearing plates, and welcoming guests.

Taps Signature Cuisine and Bar, 76 N. Old Litchfield Rd., Litchfield Park, AZ 85340; (623) 935-2037; www.tapsbars.com; American; $$. Just across Litchfield Park (it's an actual park, not to be confused with the name of the town) is a row of eateries ranging from Middle Eastern to Mexican and sushi. They're all worth a visit, especially during the beautiful winter and spring seasons, but one of the best is Taps Signature Cuisine and Bar. It's a fantastic find for beer lovers with a dozen or so unique brews on tap. Don't let the word "bar" in the name deter you, though. The food at Taps is definitely above-average pub food. Order a hamburger and ask for it on a locally baked ciabatta bun (the All-American cheeseburger is simple and delicious) or the Blue Crab Romano flatbread is a great table nosh with creamy white sauce (a house specialty), grated Romano-Parmesan cheese, and lemon zest for a citrus kick.

Tomo Japanese Cuisine, 1550 N. Dysart Rd., Ste. A7-9, Goodyear, AZ 85395; (623) 935-2031; www.tomojapanesecuisine .com; Japanese; $$. There were two things that thrilled me about Tomo Japanese Cuisine's menu. The first was the "boat" section, which offers 4 different prix-fixe options, and the second was the Monkey Balls. Sometimes having an 11-year-old boy's sense of humor really pays off because the spicy tuna in these stuffed mushrooms was to die for and the fact that they're deep fried in spicy mayo is just icing on the cake. Anyway, the Kitchen Boat is a good option if you're dining with a partner. It comes with a house salad, 2 rice bowls, chicken and beef teriyaki gyoza, and plenty of tempura vegetables with tempura ice cream as dessert. The 6-piece sushi combination was a highlight of the visit. Tomo's sushi menu is robust and you'll find everything from halibut nigiri to specialty rolls like the Snow Corn, which is a California roll topped with red snapper and eel sauce.

A Touch of European Cafe, 7146 N. 57th Dr., Glendale, AZ 85301; (623) 847-7119; www.atouchofeuropeancafe.com; Polish; $$. Home-cooked and hearty is what this place is all about. Self-taught Chef/Owner Waldemar Okula dishes out meals that are on par with any Polish grandmother's. The BYOB establishment (beer or wine only) is known for its long list of signature soups that rotate daily. If you're lucky, you'll visit on a day that they're serving the sauerkraut with beans or beef goulash. The smoked kielbasa sandwich, served on ciabatta with cold sauerkraut slaw, is worth the trip itself, but bring a friend so you can try the pierogi platter that comes with a combination of 6 potato-cheese and smoked sausage pierogies sautéed with onions.

Vogue Bistro, 15411 W. Waddell Rd., Surprise, AZ 85379; (623) 544-9109; www.voguebistro.com; American and French; $$$. Navigating Vogue Bistro's menu is almost as fun as the sound Chef Aurore de Beauduy's name makes rolling off your tongue. Go ahead, try it. As the beauty and brains behind Vogue, Chef de Beauduy studied under culinary masters like Alain Sanderens and Michel Guerard. She must have hit the books hard because the food here is easy competition for some of the greats in big cities like New York and San Francisco. The menu combines the best of both worlds in American and French cooking. Sandwiches like the Croque Monsieur, a Parisian specialty ham and cheese sandwich, are show stoppers and the same goes for most of the entrees on the list, but the herb garlic jus on the roasted chicken made my night. Side dishes—labeled "Accessories" on the tongue-in-cheek menu—include vanilla butternut squash, plantains, and Chef Aurore's quiche of the day. See Chef Aurore's recipe for **Arugula Pesto with Pickled Yellow Tomatoes Bruschetta** on page (232).

Landmarks

Haus Murphy's, 5739 W. Glendale Ave., Glendale, AZ 85301; (623) 939-2480; www.hausmurphys.com; German; $$. This could very well be the best place in all of Greater Phoenix for Oktoberfest and it probably has a lot to do with the bands that they bring in, which are almost always straight from Germany. Haus Murphy's is a great place to visit any other time of year, too, thanks to its affordable menu of quality German food and beer. Opt for the Brie en Croute, 2 wedges of brie wrapped and baked in pastry dough, instead of the sausage sampler for an appetizer and order from the list of bratwurst for your main course instead. From the schnitzel list, the paprika and schweizer are real winners with German fried potatoes and a cup of soup to boot.

La Perla Cafe, 5912 W. Glendale Ave., Glendale, AZ 85301; (623) 939-7561; www.laperlacafe.net; Mexican; $$. At Glendale's La Perla Cafe, the spotlight shines on Chihuahua-style Mexican food, which is a milder, less spicy version of the New Mexican cuisine found throughout the Southwest. The restaurant opened in 1946 and is still a family-run business where, besides authentic food, you can find live mariachi entertainment on the weekends. La Perla's menu isn't particularly innovative—you'll find all of the traditional dishes like chicken mole and huevos rancheros—but that's okay because the classics are done well. If you're looking for a trendy, "scene" dining experience, skip La Perla. But if what you're looking for is down-home Mexican food where you can grab a bite in a ball cap and jeans, it's definitely worth the visit.

Pedro's Mexican Restaurant, 4938 W. Glendale Ave., Glendale, AZ 85301; (623) 937-0807; Mexican; $. Pedro's Mexican Restaurant isn't on the cutting edge of Mexican cuisine, but this mom and pop shop must be doing something right because it's been going strong in the West Valley since the 1950s. Heck, even crazy-haired crooner Rod Stewart ordered take-out from Pedro's, so if that's not enough to convince you, I don't know what is. Actually, let it be the sweet green corn tamale plate or the mix-your-own salsa bowls because, well, anything is better than Rod Stewart. On an interesting note, Pedro's also has a special low-carb dish if you're keeping count. It's shredded beef topped with sour cream and cheese with lettuce and tomato for garnish. And, in a town where you're more likely to find Kobe Bryant's Nike shoes than Steve Nash's at local sports shops, I give Pedro's extra props for showcasing Arizona sports team memorabilia on its walls.

Shish Kebab House, 5158 W. Olive Ave., Glendale, AZ 85302; (623) 937-8757; www.theshishkebabhouse.com; Greek; $$. The Shish Kebab House has been a fixture in the Valley of the Sun for about 20 years and has changed locations a few times as demand has grown. Much of its success can be attributed to the friendly and personal service. If you go in more than once, you're bound to see at least some of the same staff members and they'll most likely remember your name. A word to the wise: the decor here is clean and welcoming, but not notable by any means so if you're looking for a special night out, look elsewhere. But if casual is what you're looking for, then this is the place. The same translates into plate presentation. No fancy garnishes here but the hummus is some of the best in town, the dolmeh is served warm instead of cold for a delightful twist, and the chicken kebab, gyro, and rice combination plate is more than memorable.

The Spicery in Our 1895 Home, 7141 N. 59th Ave., Glendale, AZ 85301; (623) 937-6534; www.1895spicery.com; Tea Room; $. Originally opened in 1986, the Spicery in Our 1895 Home went through a tough time after owner Martha Campbell sold it in 2002.

In 2010, she was able to reacquire the business and bring back the afternoon tea service that had become a favorite of Glendale residents. For $22 per person, which includes tax and tip, you get a 3-course menu of your choice of sandwich (there are 4 to pick from), currant scones and shortbread, and dessert, plus tea. Entrees for the regular lunch service change daily and come with a salad.

Farm-to-Table

McClendon's Select Produce, 15888 N. 77th Ave., Peoria, AZ 85382; (866) 979-5279; www.mcclendonsselect.com. Farmer Bob McClendon's agricultural treasure trove sits on 25 acres in the middle of the West Valley's suburbs—fields saturated with watermelon, radishes, micro greens, citrus, and asparagus thrive among rows of houses, parks, and a shopping mall. Swarms of Arizona's most persnickety chefs rely on McClendon for key ingredients, including Kevin Binkley, Chris Bianco, and Nobuo Fukuda to name a few. But even if you're not an award-winning chef, you can enjoy McClendon's products at Valley-wide farmers' markets, most notably the Old Town Scottsdale one where his fresh produce is the undeniable star of the show. In fact, some 1,400 people take home McClendon's Select Produce on a weekly basis.

Seacat Gardens, 4762 North 189th Ave., Litchfield Park, AZ 85340; (623) 846-4624; www.seacatgardens.com. No one talks about heirloom tomatoes and melons with as much enthusiasm as Carl Seacat. In fact, Google "Seacat Gardens" and you'll come up with a list of videos and articles dedicated entirely to the man and his love for organic produce. His growing operation is based on one leased acre of land in Litchfield Park's larger Blue Sky Farms where he first started growing his popular heirloom tomatoes in 2008. You can find his collection of more than a dozen varieties—including a few unique bee-pollinated hybrids—at the Old Town Scottsdale Farmers' Market and Downtown Phoenix Public Market. With varieties like Black Russian, Cherokee Purple, and Snowbell, ordering is as much fun as eating. Greater Phoenix and Scottsdale restaurants using produce from Seacat Gardens include **Quiessence Restaurant** (see p. 48) and the **Cafe at MIM** (see p. 39), among others.

Specialty Stores, Markets & Producers

Crave Cupcakes, 5801 W. Glendale Ave., Glendale, AZ 85301; (602) 763-6289; www.cravecake.com. Simple, sweet, good. Never has a marketing tagline been more appropriate. The tiny boutique in downtown Glendale is a mecca of treats and sweets with cookies and brownies also on the menu. But I recommend getting right down to business and going directly to the cupcakes. Flavors range from traditional red velvet to s'mores with a different featured cupcake every day. I happened to visit on the glorious day of Butterfinger, now a national holiday in my book, and am still dreaming about the gooey dark chocolate cake with sweet vanilla butter cream and chocolate ganache shell.

The Wigwam Farmers' Market, 300 E. Wigwam Blvd., Litchfield Park, AZ 85340; (623) 935-3811; www.wigwamarizona.com. The market is held on the lush front lawn of the Wigwam Resort. Couple that scene with the mid-70s winter temperatures for which Phoenix is known and you're in for a magical afternoon. The Wigwam Farmers' Market is held every Sunday from October to April and has a respectable list of local vendors. Stop by Duncan Family Farms for certified organic produce or Arizona Delights for waffle cookies. And, like any good Arizona farmers' market, there's a tamale stand with order-and-eat tamales.

East Valley

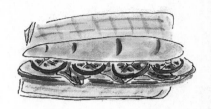

A renewed interest in "eating local" has made the East Valley Greater Phoenix's top spot for agritourism, yet many people may not realize that the area's soil is as rich as California's San Joaquin Valley.

In fact, agriculture was the major industry here until the population and structural boom of the 1950s and '60s. As luck (or genius) would have it, that's exactly when the Johnston family purchased the 160 acres in Gilbert now known as Agritopia. This mixed-use development is centered on a community garden and is unique because it combines residential, retail, and commercial space with two restaurants: Joe's Farm Grill and the Coffee Shop (both of which were featured on the Food Network).

Besides Agritopia, you'll also find the 28-acre dairy farm, Superstition Farms, in Mesa that's more like a mini amusement park with tractor rides, a "locavore" dinner series, and a farmers' market. And in Queen Creek, a once small olive mill now boasts 2,000 trees known for producing the area's best extra virgin olive oil. Not exactly a barren desert, is it?

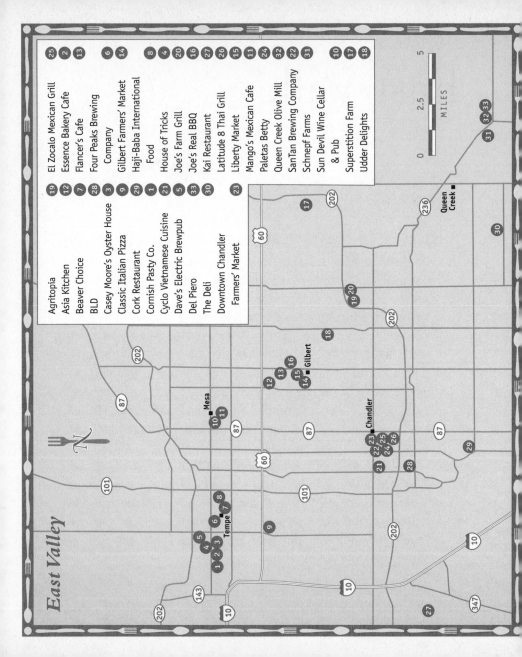

East Valley

Agritopia 19
Asia Kitchen 12
Beaver Choice 7
BLD 28
Casey Moore's Oyster House 3
Classic Italian Pizza 9
Cork Restaurant 29
Cornish Pasty Co. 1
Cyclo Vietnamese Cuisine 21
Dave's Electric Brewpub 5
Del Piero 33
The Deli 30
Downtown Chandler Farmers' Market 23

El Zocalo Mexican Grill 25
Essence Bakery Cafe 2
Flancer's Cafe 13
Four Peaks Brewing Company 6
Gilbert Farmers' Market 14
Haji-Baba International Food 29
House of Tricks 8
Joe's Farm Grill 4
Joe's Real BBQ 20
Kai Restaurant 16
Latitude 8 Thai Grill 27
Liberty Market 26
Mango's Mexican Cafe 15
Paletas Betty 11
Queen Creek Olive Mill 24
SanTan Brewing Company 32
Schnepf Farms 22
Sun Devil Wine Cellar & Pub 31
Superstition Farm 10
Udder Delights 17
18

MILES
0   2.5   5

And while the East Valley's farm belt is a major draw, Tempe's Mill Avenue District is a welcome "city" complement with Arizona State University's main campus, pedestrian-friendly downtown, and Tempe Town Lake for urban water recreation enthusiasts.

Oftentimes, when I'm around town, I hear non–East Valley residents say things like: "I never thought I'd be able to get authentic Thai food in Chandler," or, my personal favorite: "I heard that they have really good restaurants in Mesa, but that you can't get alcohol anywhere."

Hopefully, my exaggerated sigh somehow translates through the pages of this book.

You can't blame these folks for having preconceived notions. The East Valley is, after all, a farming community at its core and that automatically brings to mind long stretches of nothingness. The important thing is that minds are quickly changed after one visit.

I'm a Gilbert resident so take my opinion with a grain of salt, but I'd venture to say that the East Valley's charm is more laidback and organic than other Greater Phoenix regions. It's a comparably recent extension in the Valley of the Sun where restaurants and shopping centers were built out of necessity as population grew, as opposed to the "if you build it, they will come" mentality that has been important in recent growth for the more tourism-driven communities of Phoenix and Scottsdale.

But, that doesn't make the East Valley any better or worse than the rest of Greater Phoenix. In fact, this diversity in community character is exactly what makes the Valley of the Sun work. The East Valley is just another extension of the culinary offerings.

Foodie Faves

Asia Kitchen, 1236 E. Baseline Rd., Ste. 102, Mesa, AZ 85204; (480) 892-0688; www.asiaaz.com; Asian Fusion/Sushi; $$. Asia Kitchen is a tiny space where a central open kitchen takes up at least half of the area and tables are strategically placed around its perimeter. Chinese lanterns, chalkboard walls, and dark red and black hues make it a warm space and, somehow, they even manage to fit in a jazz band on weekends. The Asian Pacific Rim menu is broken down by country—Japan, China, Vietnam, Malaysia, and Singapore—and features noodle, rice, and low-carb dishes from each. My go-to here is the Lantern Flame Flat Rice Noodles from Singapore with a spicy red sauce, shrimp, chicken, and egg. Regular sushi rolls like spicy tuna and Philly range from $3 to $9 and the most expensive specialty roll is $12—impressive prices, especially considering the quality you get here. On Saturday, happy hour starts at 12 p.m.

Beaver Choice, 1743 E. Broadway Rd., Tempe, AZ 85282; (480) 921-3137; www.beaverchoice.com; Polish/Scandinavian; $$. The atmosphere at Beaver Choice is that of a fast, casual restaurant, but know that the food here is prepared fresh per order so don't expect a complete meal in 5 minutes. Instead, take a seat at one of the Ikea brand tables (it's Scandinavian, after all!) and play some games while you wait for your order. Choose from items like Chicken Schnitzel Cordon Bleu with brie instead of swiss, traditional Swedish meatballs in cream sauce and lingonberry preserve, and Jansson's Temptation, a baked dish layered with Swedish anchovies, potatoes, onion, and heavy cream. You should also know that the quality of food means slightly higher prices than most fast casual concepts. Most dishes run from $10.25 to the $13 range.

BLD, 1920 W. Germann Rd., Chandler, AZ 85286; (480) 779-8646; www.bldchandler.com; American; $$. BLD stands for breakfast, lunch, and dinner. From the same owners as **Cork** (see p. 187), it serves, among other things, house-made charcuterie and barista-made coffee from a drive-through. Breakfast items range from the traditional buttermilk pancakes and steak and eggs to more creative dishes like the Breakfast Meat Loaf with melted mozzarella, potatoes, and egg. Lunch standouts include the citrus salad with shaved fennel, orange, grapefruit, and mint on a bed of baby arugula with a lip-smacking lemon pepper vinaigrette, and the short rib dip hoagie with roasted onions and peppers. The "build your own entree" option for dinner is a fun twist and lets you choose the protein, starch, and vegetable combination.

Classic Italian Pizza, 1030 E. Baseline Rd., Ste. 156, Tempe, AZ 85283; (480) 345-8681; www.classicitalianpizza.com; Italian; $$$. Owner Azhar Began's pies are often compared to Chris Bianco's, an association in which he takes pride. I agree it's a major compliment, but I worry that it sells Classic Italian short. The food, wine, and ambiance here are their own, and it's all done well. Plus, no 4-hour waits! Classic Italian sits under a clock tower just a few doors down from Big Lots, but Began has more than made up for a bland outer façade with an interior design that is both romantic and casual without trying too hard. The wood-burning oven turns out pizzas that are fresh and flavorful with some of the best crust in town. If you're a garlic fan (read: fanatic), order the aglio olio dip. It's a wonderfully pungent combo of chopped garlic and jalapeño in pumpkin seed oil. Classic Italian's antipasto also is my favorite in town because it reminds me of the plates of house-made meat and cheese my mother puts out for guests. Both come served with Began's signature wood-fired bread. The spicy Diavola pizza has become a personal obsession at this point: pepperoni, sausage, crushed red peppers, and fresh jalapeños. See Classic Italian Pizza's recipe for **Aglio Olio Garlic Dip** on p. 234.

HOME GROWN CHAINS: PITA JUNGLE

After a few frustrating post-graduate years sans job offers, three Arizona State University alumni pooh-poohed their advanced degrees in broadcasting and engineering, and ventured into the restaurant business. **Pita Jungle** (www.pitajungle .com), now a successful chain throughout Arizona and California, is perfect for vegetarians and foodies with a taste for fresh produce. Their ever-changing and entirely original menus reflect the season's freshest, ripest ingredients prepared with Mediterranean flair and served with a bottle of Sriracha. My Yellowfin Tuna Honey Sesame Salad was surprising and delicious, served with mangos and strawberries.

Cork Restaurant, 4991 S. Alma School Rd., Ste. 101, Chandler, AZ 85248; (480) 883-3773; www.corkrestaurant.net; American; $$$. Cork is a good spot in the East Valley for romantic dinners or special celebrations. Besides the elegant decor, another focal point is the 25-foot, floor-to-ceiling climate-controlled wine wall with more than 400 selections. *Wine Spectator* loves Cork so much that they've consistently ranked it high in their "Award of Excellence" program. Known for its small plates menu, Cork features edgy dishes like grilled foie gras with charred peaches and duck-fat poached elk loin in an almond pesto jus. On Sunday, stop in for tastes of sourdough french toast decked out in orange marmalade and poached shrimp salad. Happy hour is a good time to experience Cork's flavors in a more wallet-friendly setting with snacks and small plates ranging from $3 to $8.

Cornish Pasty Co., 960 W. University Dr., Tempe, AZ 85281; (480) 894-6261; www.cornishpastyco.com; British; $. You could describe a Cornish pasty as Britain's version of the calzone or pita. In fact, I'd describe them as a cross between that and pot pie. Pasties originated from Southwest England in the 1200s, where wives and mothers would bake the pocket-like treats for workers in the nearby tin mines. Cornish Pasty Co. in Tempe is a cult favorite of sorts in Greater Phoenix because the food is deliciously good and affordable—the restaurant's signature pasties range from $6 to $9 for a hearty serving. Go all the way and order the Royale with Cheese. It's packed with hamburger meat, french fries, grilled onions, mushrooms, bacon, cheddar, and swiss cheeses, and served with your choice of dipping sauce. There is a second location at 1941 W. Guadalupe Rd., Mesa, AZ 85202; (480) 838-3586.

Cyclo Vietnamese Cuisine, 1919 W. Chandler Blvd., Chandler, AZ 85224; (480) 963-4490; www.cycloaz.com; Vietnamese; $$. At Cyclo (pronounced sik-lo), the food packs as much of a personality as owner Justina Duong, whom you can catch walking around the restaurant and chatting up guests. The menu is a long list of lively appetizers, salads, and meat, rice, noodle, and vegetable dishes. The pho, a Vietnamese noodle soup, is what first brought me in years ago and I still order the sirloin beef version almost every time I visit. Maybe it has something to do with the DIY aspect; pho is traditionally served with a side of herbs, sprouts, chile, and lime so that you can spice up the soup to personal preference. The local *Arizona Republic* food critic raves about the rice-flour crepe with pork and shrimp any chance he gets, and the spicy beef salad is another local favorite. I would guess it has something to do with the tangy and piquant Thai chili dressing.

Dave's Electric Brewpub, 502 S. College, Tempe, AZ 85281; (480) 967-5353; www.daveselectricbrewpub.com; Brewpub; $$. If you want to see what life as an Arizona State University college student is like, visit Dave's Electric Brewpub in the fall during an ASU football game. Its convenient location across from Wells Fargo Arena makes it a favorite among ASU students and alumni but it's the Bisbee, Arizona-made microbrews that consistently rank Dave's as a top place for beer connoisseurs. Choose from lager, IPA, pale ale, and oatmeal stout. Menu items are what you would expect from a microbrew—sandwiches, wraps, burgers, and salads—but Dave's does them exceptionally well. It's the chicken wings, though, that are the real highlight. They are flash fried and then put on the grill, making for some extra crispy goodness. Flavors include buffalo, chipotle, ultimate electric hot, and more.

The Deli, 18914 E. San Tan Blvd., Queen Creek, AZ 85242; (480) 279-3546; www.thedeliqc.com; Deli/Sandwiches; $$. Blake and Nicole Mastyk of the Deli in Queen Creek are no strangers to the culinary world—he's the former chef at Cartwright's in Cave Creek and she is an experienced sommelier. Their expertise is show-

cased in a fantastic light at the Deli, where soups, salads, sandwiches, and pizza are made from locally sourced, seasonal ingredients. Weekly dinner specials highlight a meatier selection and come with optional wine pairings. Past dishes include Alaskan cod with white bean puree and braised beef short ribs in a roasted tomato ragu. You'll have trouble picking just one option from the long list of gourmet sandwiches, but the hot Italian sausage should be at the top of your list, if only for the roasted tomato aioli and fresh-baked baguette.

Del Piero, 25062 S. Meridian Rd., Queen Creek, AZ 85242; (480) 888-9290; www.queencreekolivemill.com; Italian; $$. Del Piero is a Tuscan-inspired cafe inside the **Queen Creek Olive Mill** (see p. 199) where you can indulge every craving you've ever had, from sweet to savory. For breakfast, try the vanilla bean olive oil waffles (my favorite is the berries and cream) or homemade frittatas like the egg, asiago, and herb roasted vegetable. Lunch means a wide selection of bruschetta, salads, sandwiches, and paninis. The Manzi Panini is a family recipe and is tequila-lime roasted free-range chicken breast, fontina cheese, garden basil, and Queen Creek Olive

Mill's own sun-dried tomato and Parmesan tapenade on rosemary focaccia. Treat yourself to the "That's S'More," a dessert bruschetta with fresh honey mascarpone and Nutella drizzle, and leave a happy camper.

El Zocalo Mexican Grill, 28 S. San Marcos Pl., Chandler, AZ 85225; (480) 722-0303; www.elzocalo.com; Mexican; $$. Reserve a seat on El Zocalo Mexican Grill's outdoor patio and let the sounds and flavors transport you to Mexico City, where the real El Zocalo is a 16th-century plaza that's served as the stage for thousands of festivals, political rallies, and cultural celebrations. Its lush garden is especially vibrant on weekend nights, when the twinkly lights shine bright and live Latin music fills the air. You'll want to fill up on the hot homemade chips and zesty salsa but be sure to save plenty of room for the main course. Savory dishes like chile relleno and mole de pollo are the specialty here, and you'll need room to enjoy every last bite because the portion sizes are generous. There's also a long list of tequila with more than 200 varietals.

Joe's Farm Grill, 3000 E. Ray Rd., Bldg. 1, Gilbert, AZ 85296; (480) 563-4745; www.joesfarmgrill.com; American; $$. In 2009, the Food Network's Guy Fieri discovered what Gilbert residents have known for almost 10 years: the food at Joe's Farm Grill is worth the trip from anywhere in the country. Since being featured on *Diners, Drive-ins and Dives*, Joe's Farm Grill has grown in popularity and the food still manages to deliver. Located in Gilbert's mixed-use **Agritopia** neighborhood, the restaurant sources much of its fresh produce from the nearby community garden in specialties like the fontina burger, made with roasted red pepper, grilled mushrooms, field greens, and farm-made pecan pesto. Other highlights include the fresh beet salad with toasted pecans and blue cheese, and the barbecue pork sandwich. There's also a selection of wood-fired pizzas, fries and rings, and milkshakes for dessert. Joe's Farm Grill is housed in the converted 1960s Johnston family home.

Joe's Real BBQ, 301 N. Gilbert Rd., Gilbert, AZ 85234; (480) 503-3805; www.joesrealbbq.com; Barbecue; $$. If there's one thing owner Joe Johnston knows, it's good food. I guess the other thing is creating restaurants where the atmosphere is as much of a reason to visit as the menu. Take a look at his résumé and you'll understand; he's also got a hand in **Liberty Market** (see p. 194) and **Joe's Farm Grill** (see p. 191) at **Agritopia** (see p. 199). Joe's Real BBQ is the second in that lineup after the farm grill and serves slow-cooked, pecan-wood barbecue from a 1929 brick building that evokes Arizona's "golden age" of agriculture. The outdoor patio is more like a ranch home backyard with grass, picnic tables, white picket fence, and strung twinkly lights. Meat choices include sliced beef brisket, pulled pork, turkey jalapeño sausage, and pork ribs, among others. My favorite thing about barbecue is the side dishes, and the cheesy potatoes at Joe's are a must-try.

Kai Restaurant, 5594 W. Wild Horse Pass Blvd., Chandler, AZ 85226; (602) 225-0100; www.wildhorsepassresort.com; Southwestern; $$$. Kai is the signature restaurant at Sheraton Wild Horse Pass Resort and Spa on the Gila River Indian Community, home to the Pima and Maricopa Native American tribes. Its name is the Pima word for "seed," and Executive Chef Michael O'Dowd has incorporated the spirit of the cultures into his food by using indigenous ingredients grown on the nearby Gila River farm. Kai's is a sophisticated menu where starters range from seasonal soups like the chilled melon puree to a micro greens salad with local olive oil and vegetables in a white honey lime drizzle. Main courses are even more beautifully crafted; the butter-basted lobster, shrimp, and scallops is a wonderful potpourri of seafood and pasta, heirloom tomatoes, gruyère cheese, ham, and crisp shallots. Kai is a critic's choice, too. It is Arizona's only AAA Five Diamond restaurant and has been recognized by the *Mobil Travel Guide*.

Latitude 8 Thai Grill, 11 W. Boston St., Chandler, AZ 85225; (480) 722-0560; www.latitude-eight.com; Thai; $$. Latitude 8 Thai Grill is the geographic location for the southern part of Thailand comprising the island of Phuket and coastal cities of Krabi and Hat Yai. Both here and at Latitude 8 in Chandler, seafood dominates the scene. Feasting on the seafood green curry was a tasty treasure hunt of king crab, mussels, fish, shrimp, scallops, and squid, and the seared ahi with Phuket sauce was a beautiful mashup of grilled asparagus and yellow and red curry with whipped potatoes. A dessert of fried plantains is enough to bring you back a second time. They are coconut battered and served with tangy Kaffir lime syrup. Latitude 8's food pairs well with its wine selection and there's also a nice collection of Asian beers and tea.

Liberty Market, 230 N. Gilbert Rd., Gilbert, AZ 85234; (480) 892-1900; www.libertymarket.com; Cafe Fare; $$. When the original Liberty Market opened its doors in 1935, Gilbert was still a small farming community with a population of roughly 800 people. What was once a family-run grocery store is now a (still family-run) restaurant and specialty market serving everything from wood-fired pizza to grilled sandwiches and fresh fish entrees. Popular items are starred on the menu, like the Best Chicken Sandwich, with Monterey Jack, spicy avocado spread, and chipotle vinaigrette. Liberty Market's espresso bar is one of the best in town, too, and features unique drinks like a Cuban micro-latte and Ca Phé, a Vietnamese coffee. Take a seat at the bar and order one with a blueberry or cranberry scone. They're served with a homemade extra-whipped cream that is light and not too sweet. Owners Kiersten and David Traina (who is also the chef) tend their own garden plot at **Agritopia** (see p. 199), where they grow much of Liberty Market's produce. See Kiersten Traina's recipe for **Chicken Pasta in a Parmesan Thyme Sauce** on p. 246.

Mango's Mexican Cafe, 44 W. Main St., Mesa, AZ 85201; (480) 464-5700; www.mangosmexicancafe.com; Mexican; $. Downtown Mesa is rich in independent restaurants and shops like Mango's Mexican Cafe. This cozy eatery has a collection of *agua frescas* on tap that are made from fresh fruit like cantaloupe, lemon, and watermelon, and are perfect for a warm day. The casual restaurant has a bright and cheery atmosphere with a menu that's all about comfort: tacos, chimis, and nachos—the gang's all here. Guacamole, salsa, and crunchy chips are made fresh daily and it's one of the few places where a veggie burrito is actually worth the money. My favorite of the trip was the shredded chicken enchilada. It's a simple dish but the gooey cheese and zesty red sauce made it memorable.

SanTan Brewing Company, 8 S. San Marcos Place, Chandler, AZ 85225; (480) 917-8700; www.santanbrewing.com; Brewery; $$. SanTan Brewing Company in downtown Chandler combines craft beer with above-average bar food like brewpub pizzas, soups and salads, hamburgers, and handcrafted sandwiches. Try one of the signature burgers, like the beef patty stuffed with mozzarella, beer braised onions, and marinated mushrooms. Soft pub pretzels combine the brew with food in the best possible way: beer mustard and cheese for dipping. SanTan's core beers like HopShock I.P.A and Hefeweizen Wheat are always on tap and brew master Anthony Canecchia keeps things fresh with specialty seasonal and small batch beer. For deal seekers, SanTan's happy hour touts $3.75 pints and $5 select appetizers. Its lively pub-like atmosphere and spacious outdoor patio make it a good option for groups.

Landmarks

Casey Moore's Oyster House, 850 S. Ash Ave., Tempe, AZ 85281; (480) 968-9935; www.caseymoores.com; Gastropub; $$. You could classify Casey Moore's as Tempe's unofficial, official hipster hangout. The restaurant dishes out seafood, beef, and chicken selections from a historic home in a neighborhood near Arizona State University. Oh, and it's quite possibly haunted by the ghost of the woman who once lived there. Interested yet? If that's not enough, the crispy fish and chips or open-faced tuna bacon melt should be. Dinner selections are slightly pricier than the menu's salads and sandwiches but come with choice of soup or salad and rice pilaf or double-baked potato. Spicy tomato sauce in the Cioppino of Seafood dish was fresh and flavorful over a bed of linguine and shrimp, and the chicken pesto with sun-dried tomatoes was another table favorite. Casey's turns into more of bar scene after 9 p.m. and you'll find many of the same nighttime visitors nursing hangovers with comfort food and mimosas the next day.

Flancer's Cafe, 610 N. Gilbert Rd., Ste. 300, Gilbert, AZ 85234; (480) 926-9077; www.flancers.com; Cafe Fare; $$. Three words every sandwich enthusiast wants to hear: fresh-baked bread. Sure, many restaurants claim their bread is made on site—and that might be true—but the difference between them and Flancer's is that this restaurant in Gilbert actually makes their own dough and bakes it fresh. You won't go wrong with any of the sandwiches on the menu, but two favorites are the Parmesana Nirvana Chicken (you can get it with meatball or eggplant, too) and the Tradition! Tradition! Reuben. Locals love Flancer's because of their generous happy hour. It's daily from 3 to 7 p.m. and offers $1 off all beer, wine, and spirits, plus food specials.

Four Peaks Brewing Company, 1340 E. 8th St., Ste. 104, Tempe, AZ 85281; (480) 303-9967; www.fourpeaks.com; Brewery; $$. Four Peaks Brewing Company is a great place to kick back with a cold one on game day or any day of the week, for that matter. Set in a building originally constructed in 1892, its Mission Revival style has remained intact over years of renovations with redbrick walls and a wooden ceiling that add a touch of funky warehouse atmosphere. Go for the handcrafted ales (Arizona Peach is great in the warmer months!) and the food. Try one of Four Peaks' signature beer bread sandwiches, which is like a fluffier, denser version of pita bread. The grilled chicken is a flavorful medley of artichoke, mushroom, green pepper, and red onion with a refreshing cucumber sauce. Four

Peaks makes the beer selection easier by including recommended pairings with menu items. There is a second location at 15730 N. Pima Rd., Ste. D5-7, Scottsdale, AZ 85260, (480) 991-1795.

House of Tricks, 114 E. 7th St., Tempe, AZ 85281; (480) 968-1114; www.houseoftricks.com; French and American; $$$. Since 1987, House of Tricks has been a staple on Greater Phoenix's fine dining scene. It's spread between two early 1900s bungalow homes in a romantic setting complete with white twinkle lights, and a lush garden of green ferns and bright red flowers that's tended by owner Bob Trick's mother. The interior space is small but that's okay because the outdoor patio is really where you'll want to be. (Bonus: It's also where the bar is!) Chef Kelly Fletcher's cuisine is both consistent in quality and innovative in design. Chipotle-watermelon barbecue sauce drew me to order the braised short ribs, and the goat cheese potato puree that came with it was deliciously decadent. Even vegetarian options at House of Tricks are worth the trip, especially the goat cheese lasagna in an organic basil-walnut pesto. Fun fact: The inside walls are a makeshift art exhibit with works from internationally recognized artists like Mark Klett and Aaron Fink.

Agritopia, 3000 E. Ray Rd., Gilbert, AZ 85296; (480) 988-1238; www.agritopia.com. The utopian community of Agritopia is an experiment in living simply where residential, commercial, and retail space is packed into 160 acres around an urban farm called the Community Garden. Area residents aren't the only ones taking notice; Valley chefs like David Traina of **Liberty Market** (see p. 194) grow their own produce here, too. Stop by for a stroll through the garden and to dine at **Joe's Farm Grill** (see p. 191) or grab an espresso and sweet treat from the **Coffee Shop**, whose owners were featured on an episode of *Cupcake Wars*. The banana cream pie is a must-try, too, and you won't be able to leave without a stop at the farm stand for a doggie bag of the garden's latest harvest.

Queen Creek Olive Mill, 25062 S. Meridian Rd., Queen Creek, AZ 85242; (480) 888-9290; www.queencreekolivemill.com. Owner Perry Rea took the skills he learned working in Detroit's automotive industry and focused them onto a different kind of oil—olive. Queen Creek Olive Mill started as a small farm and grew to an operation of 2,000 trees that produce the area's best-known extra virgin olive oil. Five dollars will get you onto a behind-the-scenes tour with a rundown on the mill's history, a look at how signature oils are made, and a taste of several oils, vinegars, stuffed olives, and tapenades—all of which are available for purchase in the gourmet marketplace. Snag some of the strategically placed recipe cards for instructions on how to put the goods to work at home. There's also a Tuscan-inspired eatery, **Del Piero**, and regular special events with wine tastings and live music in the grove.

Schnepf Farms, 22601 E. Cloud Rd., Queen Creek, AZ 85242; (480) 987-3100; www.schnepffarms.com. Schnepf Farms is a year-round agricultural playground where you can wander budding peach groves and U-pick veggie stations; enjoy alfresco Dinners Down the Orchard led by top Valley chefs; and take in the sights, sounds, and smells of a chili cook-off and pumpkin festival—all dependent on the time of year. Stop by the country store and bakery in the farm's roadside stand for fresh baked cinnamon rolls, muffins, garden fresh salads, chili, and soup. On weekends, the farm is a family retreat with hay and train rides, and a petting zoo, carousel, and playground. And be sure to visit the 100-year-old farmhouse, the original Schnepf family home that now acts as a museum.

Superstition Farm, 3440 S. Hawes Rd., Mesa, AZ 85209; (602) 432-6865; www.superstitionfarmtours.com. Hop on a hayride at Superstition Farm in Mesa to take in the 55 acres that include an all-rescue petting zoo, ice cream at the Milk Bar, and a farm store with fresh eggs, cheese, and butter. On Thursday, Superstition hosts an indoor farmers' market from 4:30 to 7:30 p.m. where you can pick up your fresh seafood, vegetables, honey, and bread, then make dinner on the spot using one of the farm's open grills. Mooster's Mootique is an Urban Outfitters–meets–roadside stand gift shop of toys, games, candy, and clothes for the little ones. It was built using only recycled material with insulation made from used blue jeans.

Specialty Stores, Markets & Producers

Downtown Chandler Farmers' Market, Dr. A.J. Chandler Park, 3 S. Arizona Ave., Chandler, AZ 85225. Every Thursday in October through May from 3 to 7 p.m., the Downtown Chandler Farmers' Market brings about 40 local vendors and purveyors to the Dr. A.J. Chandler Park. This market's startup could be the most "organic" of them all; it began as a one-man show when Jeff Scott of Jeff Scott Farms in Willcox would set up a farm stand in the park after his weekly restaurant deliveries. Other vendors took notice and the market quickly grew into an official event sponsored by the downtown group. You can still find fresh produce from Jeff Scott Farms, along with goods from downtown Chandler businesses like handcrafted Mexican ice pops from **Paletas Betty** (see p. 205) and award-winning barbecue sauce from **Freddie G's**. Other vendors sell fresh and prepared foods (try the tamales!), soaps, jewelry, and clothing, and there is new entertainment every other week like live musicians, face painting, kids' activities, and more.

Essence Bakery Cafe, 825 W. University Dr., Tempe, AZ 85281; (480) 966-2745; www.essencebakery.com. For a woman with such a complicated last name, Chef/Owner Eugenia Theodosopoulos sure has mastered the art of simplicity. And the *macaron*, for that matter. No, not macaroon—*macaron* with one O. The sandwich-like French pastry is basically God's gift to dessert lovers: It's a filling of either chocolate ganache or flavored pastry cream slotted between two domed cookies similar in texture to baked meringue, just chewier. They come in flavors like French chocolate, caramel, and strawberries and cream. As if that weren't enough of a heavenly experience,

Theodosopoulos also tempts your sweet tooth with delicate petit fours, cinnamon butter muffins, and miniature cakes. The treats are what brought me in but I was happily surprised to see a menu of salads and sandwiches made with produce from McClendon Farms, grass-fed beef from Power Ranch in southeastern Arizona, and olive oil from **Queen Creek Olive Mill** (see p. 199).

Gilbert Farmers' Market, 222 N. Ash St., Gilbert, AZ 85234; (480) 332-3030; www.gilbertfarmersmarket.com. The day I found out Gilbert was finally getting a farmers' market was, quite frankly, one of the best days of my life. My sad, unexciting personal existence aside, seeing it develop from little more than 10 vendors into a full-blown agricultural extravaganza has been a real treat. You'll find fresh heirloom tomatoes, organic eggs, Arizona cheese and apple butter, gelato, local honey, artisan sea salt, grass-fed local beef, tea, gourmet popcorn and coffee, and so much more. If the idea of flying home with a packed suitcase of souvenirs makes you itch, plan a visit to Gilbert Farmers' Market for the **Sunshine & Spice** and **Superstition Farm** (see p. 201) food trucks. Quiche, omelets, rotisserie chicken, baked beans, and corn bread are just some of the past menu items. The Gilbert Farmers' Market takes place every Saturday morning and specific times vary by season.

Home Grown Chains: Serrano's Fine Mexican Food Restaurants

Cheese plays a deeply significant role in my life. When cheese is melted and churned with spinach in a spicy *pico de gallo* and served to me with tortilla chips in a stylish black booth amidst an upscale but relaxing dining experience, I tend to gush without pausing for sentence breaks. The Serrano family operates 8 restaurant locations throughout Arizona, including 7 **Serrano's Mexican Restaurants** (www.serranosaz.com) and 1 **Brunchies** in Downtown Chandler, open for (you guessed it) brunch every day until midafternoon.

Haji-Baba International Food, 1513 E. Apache Blvd., Tempe, AZ 85281; (480) 894-1905; www.haji-baba.com. Haji-Baba's wholesale operation distributes 3,000 specialty food products from the Middle East, India, and Europe to hotels, grocers, restaurants, food vendors, and caterers in the Greater Phoenix area. Its small retail shop in Tempe is the first place I remember going shopping as a kid with my parents. We'd make out like bandits with Croatian cookies, preserves, candies, and meat. Haji-Baba gave them the small taste of home that so many freshly minted US citizens crave, and it gave me, well, chocolate wafer cookies that I would have gladly strapped to my neck with a feedbag. There's a restaurant side to Haji-Baba, too, with gyros, hummus, taboule, schwarma, kebabs, and Turkish coffee. Oh, and in case you're wondering, those fruit-of-life wafer cookies are called "napolitanke." Buy a box and just try to resist polishing it off in one sitting.

Paletas Betty, 96 W. Boston St., Ste. 100, Chandler, AZ 85225; (480) 779-8080; www.paletasbetty.com. A *paleta* is a handmade Mexican ice pop and the ones at Paletas Betty in downtown Chandler are especially delicious because they don't use any canned or frozen fruits, or artificial preservatives and coloring. Spices are ground fresh from whole pieces and everything is made entirely from scratch. Because they use seasonal ingredients, flavors change on a regular basis but if you see either the San Valentin or Mango con Chile on the menu, try them! The first is a simple but delicious strawberry pop covered in dark chocolate and the latter, a more adventurous combination of sweet mango and handmade chile powder. The pops are crafted in molds made to look like someone's already taken a bite, a cute touch but I'd rather have the extra ice-cream mass!

Sun Devil Wine Cellar & Pub, 235 N. Country Club Dr., Mesa, AZ 85201; (480) 834-5050; www.topsliquors.com. Tucked into the corner of Sun Devil Liquors' basement is Sun Devil Wine Cellar & Pub that features a rotating variety of craft beer and microbrews, and wines by the glass. Stop by around happy hour for wine and beer tastings paired with artisan cheese and salami. Thursday and

Saturday bring live music from local acts. Stroll through rows of wine from Chile to Germany and Australia, but don't leave without a bottle of Arizona wine. You'll find labels like Arizona Stronghold, Pillsbury, and Dribble Creek. A word to the wise: Time is practically non-existent in this place thanks to the absence of windows and outdoor light. This, along with deep red walls and curtains, gives it a speakeasy feel.

Udder Delights, 1385 E. Warner Rd., Ste. 103, Gilbert, AZ 85296; (480) 507-3859; www.udderdelightsaz.com. Udder Delights is the retail extension of **Superstition Farm** (see p. 201) where you can find handmade farmer's cheese, artisan butter, cheese-infused desserts, and some of the wackiest but most delectable ice-cream flavor combinations you could ever imagine like lemon fennel and coconut lime ricotta. Yes, there are traditional tastes like strawberry, chocolate, and vanilla, but is that really what you want to order when the Superstition Farm flavor is on the menu? It's fit for a chocolate fiend and made from chocolate, cocoa, hazelnut, and Nutella. The milkshakes here are a Valley favorite and have received several local awards. Don't expect to pay the same price you would at a chain ice-cream shop, though. Udder Delight's prices are what they are because the ingredients are fresh, local, and not mass-produced. It's worth it!

Brews, Barrels & Blends: Booze in the Desert

Greater Phoenix and Scottsdale's rise in the world of cocktails correlates almost exactly to its evolution in dining. As demand for innovative, fresh cuisine grew, so too did the petitions for creative concoctions that blended more than just too-sugary syrups with well liquor. Lucky for us, master mixologists like Bill DeGroot were there to answer the call with flavorful drinks that are as much about presentation as they are about fresh, farm-to-table ingredients. DeGroot is a 15-year veteran of the local cocktail scene whose most recent work as a consultant at Quiessence Restaurant makes use of the abundant ingredients available on the restaurant's neighboring farms.

Jason Asher was the first bartender ever to make *GQ* magazine's cover in 2010 when the publication named him the country's

"Most Inspired Bartender" for his work at Sanctuary on Camelback Mountain's Jade Bar, specifically for the now-famous beet and yuzu gimlet. He's since revamped the drink menu at Magnum's Cigars, Wine and Spirits to reflect the culinary sensibility and flair he's known for. If you are lucky enough to order a drink from either of these fellas, do what any good foodie would do and ditch the menu. You won't regret putting your cocktail experience into their masterful hands.

In 1997, Four Peaks Brewing Company opened its first location in Tempe, bringing the craft beer experience to Greater Phoenix. What started as a small operation grew into a full-blown portfolio of eight flavors, the most notable of which is a Scottish-style ale

called Kiltlifter whose amber color and malty sweetness made Four Peaks a household name. Today, the company's brews can be found not only at their two Valley locations, but also in restaurants across Arizona. And approximately 10 years after Four Peaks opened its doors, SanTan Brewery in downtown Chandler popped up with a dose of healthy competition and a series of year-round, seasonal, and small batch beers. Together, these two spots inspired the onslaught of microbreweries and brewpubs that dot Greater Phoenix and Scottsdale's modern-day bar scene.

But the bevvie fun doesn't end with cocktails and craft beer. With 45 licensed and bonded wineries across the state, Arizona has undergone a transformation in recent years from an underground oenophile retreat to an all-out acclaimed wine destination. In fact, local labels have graced everything from the pages of *Wine Spectator* magazine to the exclusive tables at White House dinners.

While Spanish missionaries first started wine production in Arizona in the 1700s, the state's current industry got its start in 1973 in Sonoita, a small town bordering the southern edge. Most of the vineyards can be found here and in Elgin, or in the greater Willcox region to the southeast and up in Northern Arizona's Verde Valley. Urbanites get their fix at in-town restaurants like Scottsdale's FnB where owner Pavle Milic has made local brands like Pillsbury and Arizona Stronghold the focal point of his renowned wine list.

This chapter is dedicated to the best places in Greater Phoenix and Scottsdale for a sip of mind-blowing mélanges, memorable craft beers, and striking Arizona wines. Cheers!

Cocktail & Wine Bars

AZ/88, 7353 Scottsdale Mall, Scottsdale, AZ 85251; (480) 994-5576; www.az88.com. Martinis are great, aren't they? No matter what your choice flavor—sweet, bitter, sour—there's a martini out there for you. Finding your perfect mixture is easy at AZ/88. This hip Scottsdale dinner/nightlife spot has a long list of signature martinis, like the ultra-girly but oh-so-delicious French. It's made with Absolut Kurrant vodka, Framboise liqueur, and pineapple juice. The Rose is another eye-catcher with Pinky vodka, rose nectar, lemon and lime, and a touch of Champagne. Scottsdale's finest love sipping these and other classic cocktails like Caipirinhas and Moscow Mules at this ultra-modern restaurant and lounge where the interior features an always-evolving art installation.

Beckett's Table, 3717 E. Indian School Rd., Phoenix, AZ 85018; (602) 954-1700; www.beckettstable.com. At Beckett's Table, the seasonal and homey philosophy isn't reserved just for the food. It translates into the drink selection, too. Like the appetizers, sides, and entrees, cocktails change seasonally to reflect only the freshest ingredients. In the spring and summer, focus is on Arizona's citrus bounty. The Palmaire has Ketel One Oranje and pomegranate juice mixed with lemonade, while the Flinn's Dilemma packs a punch with Jameson, lemonade, and muddled mint with a sugared rim. If you're not hungry for dinner, post up next to Beckett's Table's inviting bar where the selection also boasts a healthy wine list, including local labels like Pillsbury.

Carly's Bistro, 128 E. Roosevelt St., Phoenix, AZ 85004; (602) 262-2759; www.carlysbistro.com. Hipsters in Greater Phoenix and Scottsdale love Carly's Bistro because it has Lucid and St. George's Absinthe on the menu. Yes, the recently legalized *real* absinthe with wormwood. I can't stand the stuff so I visit Carly's for its martini list, specifically the rich goodness that is the Dutch Chocolate. Sure, the classic gin or vodka is a great choice, too, but you'll want to venture outside of the norm with the Cucumbertini, which is refreshing and smooth. The wine list is basic if not unimpressive but cocktails at Carly's run the gamut from sangria to prickly pear margaritas and the classic Greyhound.

Citizen Public House, 7111 E. 5th Avenue, Ste. E, Scottsdale, AZ 85251; (480) 398-4208; www.citizenpublichouse.com. Citizen Public House is a cozy, unassuming gastropub with plenty of welcoming tables but the best seat in the house is at its sleek metal bar, especially when Richie Moe is on the clock. He's a veteran of the Valley bartending scene most recognized (before moving to Citizen Public House, of course) for his work at **Cowboy Ciao** (see p. 130). He's a no-holds-barred kind of barkeep who's mixed whiskey with ginger ale, cucumber water, crushed red pepper, and a tinge of red onion—and people *liked it*. At Citizen Public House, Moe's timeless concoctions like the rye-full Sazerac and Pisco Sour steal the show.

Classic Italian Pizza, 1030 E. Baseline Rd., Ste. 156, Tempe, AZ 85283; (480) 345-8681; www.classicitalianpizza.com. Owner

Azhar Began is a culinary Renaissance man who crafts everything at Classic Italian Pizza, from the pizza crust to the well-planned wine list and cocktail menu. Unsurprisingly, Italian wines are the feature here but Began puts a lot of thought into the menu with varietals from regions like Umbria, Puglia, Sicily, and Piemonte, among others. Prices are accessible and he'll help you choose just the right wine to complement your meal, from a Venica Pinot Grigio to a medium-bodied Montepulciano that is easy to drink with notes of blackberry. The reserve list is impressive, particularly the Chianti Classic from Villa Caffagio in Tuscany. See Chef Began's recipe for **Aglio Olio Garlic Dip** on p. 234.

Down Under Wines & Bistro, 1422 W. Warner Rd., Gilbert, AZ 85233; (480) 545-9900; www.downunderwinesandbistro.com. I originally visited Down Under Wines & Bistro with the idea to review it for a listing in the restaurants section of this book but I wasn't at all thrilled with the food. The unpretentious atmosphere and live music make it a great place for a glass of wine, though. And I *loved* the tables; glass tops on oak barrels. So Dundee chic! Anyway, the wine list here is respectable with American cult favorites like Stag's Leap and Caymus Cabernet Sauvignon, and a Paso Robles red blend from Justin Winery. There's a nice list of Australian wines, of course, like the Two Hands Angel's Share Shiraz.

FEZ, 3815 N. Central Ave., Phoenix, AZ 85012; (602) 287-8700; www.fezoncentral.com. When I first read through FEZ's signature drinks list, I thought I was reading a dessert menu and actually asked our waitress for the cocktail list. But with drinks named Grapesicle and Orange Marmalade, you can't blame me, right? Right? Choose from 22 martinis, nearly 10 "rocks drinks" (with ice), and a selection of flavored margaritas, wine fusions, and craft, microbrew, and domestic brews. The watermelon or honeydew melon margaritas are fantastic on a warm day and simplistic souls will appreciate the "straight up" martini with vodka and just a touch of vermouth. FEZ's scene is a mix of business professionals from nearby Downtown Phoenix, hipsters, and fabulous Arizona jetsetters. Live and DJ-spun music events are a regular occurrence.

Jade Bar at Sanctuary on Camelback Mountain Resort and Spa; 5700 E. McDonald Dr., Paradise Valley, AZ 85253; (480) 607-2300; www.sanctuaryoncamelback.com. Jade Bar is a regular on "Best Of" lists in Greater Phoenix and Scottsdale, usually topping the ranks with titles like "Best Lobby Bar" and "Best Place for People Watching." It's an ultra sleek, ultra modern indoor/outdoor bar at Sanctuary on Camelback Mountain that's an extension of the elements restaurant kitchen with handcrafted cocktails made of fresh juice, herbs, and vegetables. Signature drinks here include the Fiery Mandarin, a spicy vodka combination of jalapeño and citrus, and the Airmail with rum, lime, honey, and Prosecco. Jade Bar makes it easy to re-create their drinks with take-home recipes, too. (Though, you should know, they're never quite the same!)

Kazimierz World Wine Bar, 7137 E. Stetson Dr., Scottsdale, AZ 85251; (480) 946-3004; www.kazbar.net. Owned by the masterminds behind **Cowboy Ciao** (see p. 130), the clandestine Kazimierz World Wine Bar in downtown Scottsdale can be tricky to find. That's because the entrance to this snazzy speakeasy is in the back, away from the main walkway that connects it to Ciao. This hidden gem has a wine list that's more than 2,000 labels long (it shares a cellar with Cowboy Ciao, too) and first stole my heart with its house shot that mixes Croatian pear liquor with Mexican brandy. Sounds crazy, but it's topped with sugar and a lime, and goes down surprisingly smooth! Kazbar is the kind of place you can really get lost in with stone walls, plush furniture, and dark nooks with candles as the only source of light. It's like the wine lover's bat cave. The 75-page wine list has varietals from Australia, France, Croatia, Greece, and more.

Mabel's on Main, 7018 E. Main St., Scottsdale, AZ 85251; (480) 369-3665; www.mabelsonmain.com. Mabel's on Main oozes a *Mad Men*-esque sex appeal that no other wannabe speakeasy in the Valley has yet mastered. It's a small space with worn brick walls, elaborate wallpaper, sleek oversized leather booths, and Victorian sofas perched ever-so-coolly under sparkling chandeliers. Mabel's on Main is the kind of place that will make you want to sip on expensive cognac or a Sazerac and, lucky for your inner Don Draper or Peggy Olson, there's plenty of both on the drink menu. The place gets packed with the "beautiful people" almost every evening, so get there around 5 p.m. to guarantee some elbow room. By the time the live music starts, you'll be in a good spot.

Magnum's Cigars, Wine & Liquor, 731 E. Union Hills Dr., Ste. B10, Phoenix, AZ 85024; (602) 493-8977; www.magnumscigar wineliquor.com. Magnum's Cigars, Wine & Liquor is a man's hangout with a 450-square-foot, walk-in humidor boasting a vast collection of more than 100 fine cigars from around the world. The adjoining lounge is the perfect place to kick back with a stogie and glass of single-malt whiskey or tequila. Magnum's liquor menu runs almost 12 pages with everything from a 25-year-old Caol Ila to Artillero Reposado and the lounge also features regular tasting events and live music from local bands. Cocktails here are an ode to the golden days with traditional options like the Manhattan, and staff will even pair your chosen cigar with the right drink.

Merc Bar, 2525 E. Camelback Rd., Phoenix, AZ 85016; (602) 508-9449; www.mercbar.com. Blink and you might miss Merc Bar. This cosmopolitan-cool lounge has an unmarked doorway that leads to a martini lover's haven with a bar dishing out standard Belvedere vodka versions in addition to swankier sips like espresso, lemon drop, and vanilla flavors. Merc Bar has been designated as "a little piece of Manhattan in the Sonoran Desert," and, in fact, its sister location is in New York City. That might have something to do with its luxe ambiance. Merc Bar is the exact opposite of a place like, say, the **Hidden House** (see p. 226). It's no dive. Men here wear suits and the ladies come dressed in their finest cocktail dresses.

The Mint, 7373 E. Camelback Rd., Scottsdale, AZ 85251; (480) 947-6468; www.themintaz.com. The Mint occupies a 7,000-square-foot space in Scottsdale that used to be a bank. Staying true to its past, the focal point of its new design is the original vault door. Decor here is as rich and flashy as the bank's old clients must have been: dark wood, cohiba marble, and even a Champagne bar in the co-ed restroom. The lounge's drink selection gets in on the themed fun with selections like the Gold Digger, fortified with St. Germain elderflower liqueur, Beefeater gin, lemon, and strawberry. There's also a nice food scene courtesy of Chef Johnny Chu of Downtown Phoenix's **Sens Asian Tapas** (see p. 84). He's crafted a selective menu of dim sum and small sharing plates.

Modern Steak, 7014 E. Camelback Rd., Ste. 1433, Scottsdale, AZ 85251; (480) 423-7000; www.foxrc .com/modern_steak. If diamonds are a girl's best friend, then cocktails are her steamy love affair and Modern Steak is the sexy rendezvous spot. This place definitely caters to the girls' night out crowd with a design that looks like it was created for the modern day, sassier version of a Disney princess. It's one of the best places in town to nurture your innermost girly cocktail cravings. The Retail

Therapy is a tastier, cheaper alternative to shopper's addiction with Belvedere vodka, Grand Marnier, and strawberries. This femme fatale of drinks is joined by sisters like the Sour Cherry Fix, a tasty blend of lemon, sour cherry jam, and Vox vodka.

Narcisse Champagne & Tea Lounge, 15257 N. Scottsdale Rd., Scottsdale, AZ 85260; (480) 588-2244; www.narcisse lounge.com. Narcisse Champagne & Tea Lounge is a great nightlife option if you're traveling to Scottsdale for a bachelorette party or girlfriend getaway. Ideal for large groups of women for daytime tea or late-night bubbly, Narcisse's tables and dance floor are always packed with the Valley of the Sun's beautiful crowd. Floral and fruity cocktails match the pink-lit women's restroom and dripping diamond chandeliers for a setting that is all at once feminine, flirty, and sophisticated. If you're a high-roller, you'll rejoice in Narcisse's selection of reserve bottles like the Armand de Brignac "Ace of Spades" brut that sells for $150 per bottle. Not to worry, though—there are more affordable options with glasses of Poema Cava starting at $7. The tea-nis are a fun, herb-based twist on the regular martini. Try the lavender citrus with sparkling Mumm cuvee.

Parc Central, 15323 N. Scottsdale Rd., Scottsdale, AZ 85260; (480) 907-5333; www.parccentralrestaurants.com. Parc Central breaks its beer menu into easy-to-navigate flavor categories like "crisp and clean" and "wheaty and yeasty." Admittedly, the latter classification kind of made me cringe but, once I got over that, I was able to enjoy Parc Central for what it is: a fun, New York–like spot centered on specialty cocktails and hand-crafted martinis. The Ophelia was a flirty standout with Chambord vodka, St. Germain elderflower, cherry, and lemon juice while the Death of Marat was a put-hair-on-your-chest concoction of Absinthe, Cointreau, cognac, and lemon. On Thursday, Friday, and Saturday nights, Parc Central hosts live music. Show up early for happy hour and take advantage of $5 cocktails and wine.

Posh Scottsdale, 7167 E. Rancho Vista Dr., Scottsdale, AZ 85251; (480) 663-7674; www.poshscottsdale.com. Posh Scottsdale is one of Greater Phoenix and Scottsdale's most celebrated restaurants focusing on improvisational cuisine, but the cocktail list is as much of a reason to add it to your must-try list. Chef Joshua Hebert puts as much time and effort into the libations as he does the food. As a girl who's constantly struggling to decide between dessert and an extra cocktail, the Strawberry Shortcake Moscow Mule was a heaven-sent treat. Strawberry puree and simple syrup are fused with Russian Standard vodka and ginger beer in this drink that's the best of both worlds. An added dollop of whipped cream and strawberry for garnish are just icing on the cocktail cake. Like Posh's dining menu, its list of cocktails is constantly evolving based on seasonal ingredients.

RnR, 3737 N. Scottsdale Rd., Scottsdale, AZ 85251; (480) 945-3353; www.rnrscottsdale.com. RnR is owned and operated by Evening Entertainment Group, the Scottsdale-based nightlife experts behind daring dance clubs like **Myst** and **Axis/Radius.** So it's safe to assume these people know a thing or two about drinks. Open for breakfast, lunch, dinner, and late night, you could spend almost an entire 24 hours at RnR and not get bored. Of course, it could have something to do with the full bar, craft beers, and muddled alcoholic mixtures. Weekend brunch is prime time for people-watching, and $25 will get you bottomless Bloody Marys and mimosas. Heck, make a day of it and move into a nice afternoon of day drinking with the Stigmata Caipiroska. It's a cooling 2 shots of Absolut Acai Berry vodka and a heap of blueberries, raspberries, and strawberries, with a teaspoon of sugar and splash of cranberry and lime juices.

Shade at W Scottsdale, 7277 E. Camelback Rd., Scottsdale, AZ 85251; (480) 970-2100; www.wscottsdalehotel.com. When the W Scottsdale opened in 2008, it added 3 new fashionable bars to the Valley of the Sun's nightlife scene. One of those is Shade at W Scottsdale, the hotel's rooftop Miami-inspired destination bar. Eye-catching design includes a cascading waterfall with a candle mirage of sorts that makes it look like they're floating. The owners paid a pretty penny for the crafty fruit juicer—$3,000, to be exact—so it's no wonder that Shade's cocktails make good use of freshly squeezed produce. The Vitamin W is Shade's best selling. It's a mix of Grey Goose L'Orange, muddled raspberries, DeKuyper raspberry liqueur, and orange, cranberry, and lime.

Soi 4 Bangkok, 8787 N. Scottsdale Rd., Ste. 104, Scottsdale, AZ 85253; (480) 778-1999; www.soifour.com. Soi 4 Bangkok's name evokes a famous nightlife district in the Thai capital—*soi* means side street—and it's a posh spot that fits perfectly in Scottsdale's trendy nightlife scene. It's chock full of glamour; sculptural modern lighting, refurbished midcentury school chairs, and colorful throw pillows brighten the space that was once a cavernous strip mall block. Draft beers are the typical Stella Artois and Hoegarden selections, but bottled beer is all about the motherland with lagers straight from Thailand and Singapore. The same goes for Soi's signature drinks. Both the Basil Bliss and Ginger Drop are popular. The first is a medley of basil leaves, Tierras Anejo, and orange liqueur, while the second is a less complex but equally delicious blend of ginger, citron vodka, and fresh lime.

Wildfish Seafood Grille, 7135 E. Camelback Rd., Ste. 130, Scottsdale, AZ 85250; (480) 994-4040; www.wildfishseafoodgrille .com. Wildfish Seafood Grille is a local favorite for happy hour, especially during the slower summer months when the drink specials last all night. The Scottsdale Waterfront spot offers $2 off all drinks and specialty cocktails like mojitos, and Svedka vodka martinis are only $5. Pick up any of the local nightlife publications and you're guaranteed to see a cocktail from Wildfish Seafood Grille featured in their drink round-ups. One of the most popular is the Dragon Berry mojito.

The muddled mixture is made with fresh strawberries and dragon berry rum for a delicious and refreshing drink. On weekends, happy hour starts early at 2 p.m.

Breweries, Brewpubs & Beer Bars

Culinary Dropout, 7135 E. Camelback Rd., Ste. 125, Scottsdale, AZ 85251; (480) 970-1700; www.foxrc.com/culinary_dropout.html. I can't help laughing when I read any of Culinary Dropout's marketing material that boasts about it being a "rebel child" in the Fox Restaurant Concepts family because of their uniform-free staff and "soulful ambiance." Truth is, there's not much that's "rebellious" about this place. It's obvious that all of the details were meticulously planned, from the pretty but not-too-coiffed bartenders to the framed photos of rock idols and brand new, made-to-look-older furniture. But hey, that's not a bad thing. Culinary Dropout may cater to the pretty crowd but it's still a fun place for live music and drinks. There's a decent list of Arizona beers, brewed in places like Prescott, Flagstaff, and Chandler, as well as craft beer and timeless names like Guinness on tap. Cocktail options are a running list broken up by type of liquor, and standouts include the Jalisco Flower with tequila, elderflower, and sparkling wine, and the French Flip. It's a honey and Hennessey-based drink with lemon, egg white, and bitters.

Dave's Electric Brewpub, 502 S. College, Tempe, AZ 85281; (480) 967-5353; www.daveselectricbrewpub.com. Dave's Electric Brewpub bills itself as Arizona's first microbrewery, marking its start in history 22 years ago in Bisbee, Arizona, when the state first legalized the small operations. Taps here feature the restaurant's own beers like lager, OK Ale, and the oatmeal stouts. Its first brew, Dave's Electric IPA, remains the most popular. Its golden color glimmered beautifully in my glass on a hot summer's day and the beer finishes smooth with a nice hop flavor. Dave's Electric Brewpub is a favorite among students at nearby Arizona State University, especially during football season. It's a great option if you're looking for a laidback happy hour spot, too.

Four Peaks Brewing Company, 1340 E. 8th St., Ste. 104, Tempe, AZ 85281; (480) 303-9967; www.fourpeaks.com. Four Peaks Brewing Company has an outdoor patio that is among the most popular in the Valley of the Sun during the winter and spring seasons. Visit during any major sporting event and finding a seat anywhere in the house can be a challenge. That's because Four Peaks is an easygoing, come-as-you-are hangout with Arizona's original locally brewed beer. Its regular stable of 8 flavors include Sunbru, a German-influenced Kölsch-style ale, and the dark and dreamy Oatmeal Stout. Not that you asked, but my personal favorite is the refreshing but not-too-sweet Arizona peach ale. During the holiday season, people flock to Four Peaks in droves for the Pumpkin Porter.

The Lost Leaf, 914 N. 5th St., Phoenix, AZ 85004; (602) 258-0014; www.thelostleaf.org. Rooted in a historic Downtown Phoenix neighborhood, the Lost Leaf is built into a 1920s home that was once a butcher shop started by German immigrants. Today, the Lost Leaf is a favorite among Phoenix's artsy crowd, particularly during the First Friday art events. Its walls serve as a makeshift gallery for up-and-coming local artists to display and sell their work. Besides the crafty decor, the Lost Leaf's other highlight is the beer menu. The list features lagers, pilsners, ales, and fruity beers from not only across Arizona but also the world, including a St. Peter's Pale Ale from England and Japanese Hitachino Nest White Ale. Local beers on the menu include Nimbus Dirty Guera Hefeweizen from Tucson, Prescott Liquid Amber, and Four Peaks 8th Street Ale.

Papago Brewing, 7107 E. McDowell Rd., Scottsdale, AZ 85257; (480) 425-7439; www.papagobrewing.com. With 30 beers on tap every day, you're never short on options at Papago Brewing. In reality, this isn't always a good thing because choosing just one brew at Papago can be a challenge. So, here's my recommendation: Start with the brewery's own orange blossom ale, a light American wheat with hints of mandarin orange and vanilla. From there, well, you're on your own. Head to the tasting room where trained professionals will help you find your perfect beer, which could very well be the Trappist monk–made Chimay. It's just one of the non-Arizona craft beers you'll find on tap. Check out the large refrigerator case before you leave and take home some tasty souvenirs.

SanTan Brewing Company, 8 S. San Marcos Plaza, Chandler, AZ 85225; (480) 917-8700; www.santanbrewing.com. Anthony Canecchia, the "brew master" and owner behind SanTan Brewing, honed his skills at nearby **Four Peaks Brewing Company** (see p. 222) before opening his downtown Chandler spot in 2007. His bimonthly beer and food tastings feature SanTan's own hand-crafted brews, like the Hefeweizen Wheat and HopShock IPA, as well as American and European craft beer legends. Happy hour starts early at SanTan, at 2 p.m., and runs until 6 p.m. with a reverse happy hour beginning at 10 p.m. Monday nights are especially fun with Movie Night Specials. SanTan Brewing Company shells out $3.75 pints, popcorn, and the latest DVD releases.

Sleepy Dog Brewing, 1920 E. University Dr., Ste. 104, Tempe, AZ 85281; (480) 967-5476; www.sleepydogbrewing.com. Sleepy Dog is a production brewery that uses United States–grown malt, traditional yeast strains, and hops in its line of unique ales. It's a small but comfortable spot with vibrant green walls and a friendly staff that will walk you through the tasting process and even order you food for delivery (since it's a production brewery, noshes are really light with options like hummus and chips and salsa). Brews start with the light and crisp American lager, flowing into slightly deeper flavors like the dark Hefeweizen and a rich, creamy milk stout. Occasionally, Sleepy Dog will brew half-barrel beers in special flavors like vanilla chocolate porter and honey lager.

SunUp Brewing Co., 322 E. Camelback Rd., Phoenix, AZ 85012; (602) 279-8909; www.sunupbrewing.com. SunUp Brewing Co.'s small but mighty on-site microbrewery turns out unique brews like vanilla porter, Light Rail cream ale, and Trooper IPA, which packs a mighty 6.2 percent alcohol content. At Christmas time, SunUp Brewing Co.'s Nut Before Christmas is a popular gift that, I'm willing to bet, oftentimes doesn't make it under the tree. Unlike other establishments of its kind in Greater Phoenix and Scottsdale, SunUp Brewing didn't start with the goal of making its own beer. When the featured Sonora Brewing Company closed its doors, SunUp was faced with a choice: Close down, too, or brew their own beer. We're glad they chose the latter.

Dive Bars

Coach House, 7011 E. Indian School Rd., Scottsdale, AZ 85251; (480) 990-3433; www.coachhousescottsdale.com. Coach House is a Valley of the Sun dive bar institution. There's nothing glamorous about it—the full bar has the typical liquor and beer options, the floor is mostly dirt, and the decor is Old West chic, at best—but this is exactly why Greater Phoenix and Scottsdale residents love it. Well, that and the cheap drinks. Visit during the holiday season and you'll think, "Aw, how sweet. These lights are so festive!" In fact, the Coach House is wrapped in Christmas lights 365 days per year. As if that weren't enough to get your interest, Scottsdale's oldest bar also opens at 6 a.m. for all of your day drinking problems, er, celebrations.

The Hidden House, 607 W. Osborn Rd., Phoenix, AZ 85013; (602) 266-1763. A city is only as good as its dive bars and Greater Phoenix and Scottsdale have some of the best, including the Hidden House. This neighborhood dive has cheap drinks—domestic and well are just $2 and small pitchers are only $1 more—a dance floor, and pool tables. On Monday, Friday, and Saturday nights, DJs spin underground hip-hop and a well-stocked jukebox is on the scene as backup. A word to the wise: A deep understanding of what constitutes a "dive bar" is required before entering. There's an unmistakable tinge of stale smoke in the air.

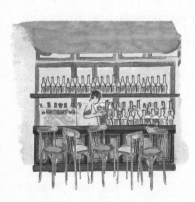

Rusty Spur Saloon, 7245 E. Main St., Scottsdale, AZ 85251; (480) 425-7787; www.rustyspursaloon.com. Rusty Spur Saloon is a small but rowdy cowboy watering hole with booming country music and peanut shell–covered floors. People pack into the spot, which was once Scottsdale's first bank but where the vaults now hold liquor instead of money, on weekends for a cold beer and some two-stepping, and the crowd is a mix of real rough-n-tough cowboys, Scottsdale socialites, and pre-and-post club-goers. You'll see minidresses alongside Daisy Dukes alongside, in more than one instance, wedding and bridesmaid dresses. The saloon describes itself as one of the three happiest places in the country, along with Disneyland and Las Vegas. I'd have to agree.

Vineyards & Wineries

Kokopelli Winery, 35 W. Boston St., Chandler, AZ 85225; (480) 792-6927; www.kokopelliwinery .com. Kokopelli Winery's vineyard is actually located in southeastern Arizona but you can get direct access to their red, white, blush, and sparkling varietals at the bistro in downtown Chandler. Daily wine tastings take place from open to close with occasional special events like Italian and BBQ Blues festivals. Kokopelli's interior has a soft but rustic feel and my favorite spot in the house is on its outdoor breezeway, especially on the weekends when there is live music. And while the red and white wines—Merlot, Chardonnay, Cabernet, and all the usual players—are good, the real stars at Kokopelli are the sparkling and blush varietals, like the Desert Rose and Imperial Kir. During happy hour, both of these wines are $2 off by the glass or $5 by the bottle.

Su Vino Winery, 7035 E. Main St., Scottsdale, AZ 85251; (480) 994-8466; www.suvinowineryaz.com. Su Vino Winery is a family-owned and -operated establishment where you can blend and barrel a bottle specific to your palate. You also can play a hand in your own winemaking destiny by bottling, corking, and labeling your blend with a custom design. Wine tasting at Su Vino is a unique experience because it's not as much about the etiquette as it is the fun. Owner Cory Whalin kicks tradition to the curb and discounts rules like drinking red wine only at room temperature and keeping tastings in a specific order. You'll find everything from sweet dessert wines like the cocoa-chocolate port and Peachy Keen to tradi-tional and blended reds and whites.

Wine & Liquor Stores

AZ Wine Merchants, 7133 E. Stetson Dr., Scottsdale, AZ 85251; (480) 425-9463. What was once empty office space between **FnB Restaurant** (see p. 105) and **Kazimierz World Wine Bar** (see p. 214) is now Pavle Milic's AZ Wine Merchants, a 400-square-foot wine retailer focusing only on Arizona-grown grapes and bottled wines. On the shelves you'll find bottles from Page Springs Cellars in Cornville, Freitas and Caduceus from Cottonwood, Dribble Creek in Jerome and Willcox, and Dos Cabezas from Cochise County. Arizona wines are becoming more and more popular, even among oenophiles outside of the state, and Milic probably has a lot to do with that. He was the first restaurateur in the Valley of the Sun to focus specifically on local varietals at his restaurant, **FnB**.

Sportsman's Fine Wine & Spirits, 3205 E. Camelback Rd., Phoenix, AZ 85018; (602) 955-7739; www.sportsmanswine.com. Sportsman's Fine Wine & Spirits started as a retail-only space that's tempted local winos since the 1950s with its running list of 1,500 bottled selections. In more recent years, Sportsman's added a small wine bar wing to its shop with more than 70 wines by the glass that are organized by varietal and region. Stop by the cold case and pick out a selection of meats and cheeses, then perch up on one of the highboy tables where a Sportsman's sommelier will craft a flight around your food. Some of the more unique labels on the list include Gauthier Select Vineyards Sonoma Coast Pinot Noir and Santa Julia Mendoza Malbec.

Recipes

Arugula Pesto with Pickled Yellow Tomatoes Bruschetta

Vogue Bistro is owned by Chef Aurore de Beauduy and her husband, Roman Yasinsky. Chef de Beauduy trained under a handful of notable French chefs early in her career, like Alain Sanderens and Michel Guerard, and then graduated from Le Cordon Bleu in Paris. She's worked at various high-end resorts and upper-crust country clubs across the United States, and this taste for exemplary food comes through at Vogue Bistro. Even a somewhat simple dish, like bruschetta, comes to life with another dimension of flavor from de Beauduy.

Bruschetta Topping

1 pound arugula
1 tablespoon honey
1 head garlic
½ cup roasted walnuts

1 log of goat cheese
½ cup olive oil
1 loaf of Ciabatta bread, cut into 1-inch slices

Blanch arugula in boiling water.

Blend arugula, honey, garlic and walnuts in a food processor or blender. Set aside.

Pickled Yellow Tomatoes

½ cup sugar	1 teaspoon allspice
1 cup vinegar	1 teaspoon mustard seed
½ cup water	1 teaspoon ginger
1 teaspoon coriander seed	1 teaspoon juniper berries
1 teaspoon clove	1 bay leaf
1 teaspoon cardamom	3 yellow tomatoes, quartered

Combine all ingredients except tomatoes and bring to a boil.

Pour over the quartered tomatoes and allow to rest overnight. Remove tomatoes from the pickling solution.

Spread goat cheese onto Ciabatta slices and assemble with arugula pesto and two wedges of pickled tomatoes.

Drizzle bruschetta with olive oil.

Toast the bread to desired consistency.

Makes 2 servings.

Courtesy of Chef Aurore de Beauduy and Roman Yasinsky, owners of Vogue Bistro (p. 174)

Aglio Olio Garlic Dip

I've heard Classic Italian Pizza Owner and Chef Azhar Began compare kneading pizza dough to cuddling your significant other after a long day: Both should be done with the utmost care and attention, apparently. His crispy, thin-crust pies have been compared to those of Chris Bianco, and local and national publications have been paying attention to this place for years. Before I tasted the Aglio Olio Garlic Dip, I was an antipasto girl when it came to Classic Italian Pizza appetizers. Give me Bulgarian feta cheese and Croatian Ajvar or give me death. But one bite of this garlic lover's dream and I was hooked. Now, I just order it alongside my antipasto. Crisis happily averted.

4 cloves garlic, chopped
1 whole jalapeño, chopped

A shot (about 2 ounces) of pumpkin seed oil
Sea salt to taste

Mix garlic, jalapeño, and pumpkin seed oil together in a bowl.

Add a touch of sea salt.

Serve with a side of crispy, toasted bread for dipping.

Courtesy of Azhar Began, chef and owner of Classic Italian Pizza (p. 186)

Spicy Grilled Broccoli

Real showstopper restaurants know that what makes a place great is the quality, in-season ingredients. FnB Restaurant and Chef Charleen Badman nailed this school of thought from the beginning—good food first, everything else second. That's not to say the decor or drink list here is second-string. In fact, the exact opposite: FnB's wine list boasts all Arizona wines (the very best of them!), and cocktails here are fresh and void of too-sweet syrups. Even the design is perfectly understated, homey with just the right amount of pizzazz. I would say the only thing that's almost better than the food here is the service.

Front-of-the-house extraordinaire and part owner, Pavle Milic, treats all guests like royalty and will probably remember what you had on your very first visit when you come in the next time. (And, believe me, you'll be back.) But what makes all of this work is the fact that everything at FnB is genuine. From the warm welcome to food that's delicious and nutritious, like this recipe. No one's ever made vegetables taste this good!

Aioli

2 garlic cloves, peeled and finely chopped

Pinch of salt

2 egg yolks

1 teaspoon water

¾ cup blended oil, a combination of canola and extra virgin olive

¼ cup extra virgin olive oil

Zest and juice of 1 tangerine or Meyer lemon

¼ teaspoon freshly ground pepper

Place garlic, salt, and egg yolks in a food processor with the whisk attachment; mix well until incorporated.

Slowly dribble the blended oil into the yolk mixture and continue whisking. As the yolk absorbs the oil, the sauce will begin to thicken.

Add the extra virgin olive oil once the blended oil is used completely.

Add the zest, citrus juice, and pepper.

Taste and add more salt, citrus zest, or garlic if desired.

Broccoli

2 broccoli heads

2 tablespoons of Sambal (a garlic chili paste found in Asian markets)

¼ cup extra virgin olive oil

½ teaspoon sea salt

¼ teaspoon freshly ground pepper

½ cup toasted, salted pistachio pieces

Trim off any leaves from the broccoli.

Trim the base and peel the stalk with a peeler. If the stalks are thick, cut them lengthways into 2 or 4, so you are left with long, thinner stalks.

Bring a pot of salted water to boil. Blanch for about 3 minutes or until the broccoli is tender but still firm.

Drain in a colander, rinse well with cold water, and let dry stalk-end-up to remove as much water from the floret as possible.

In a medium-size bowl, mix Sambal, oil, salt, and pepper. Whisk until combined.

Toss broccoli until coated evenly with Sambal mixture.

Prepare a hot fire for grilling. Oil the grill well to avoid sticking.

Grill broccoli on both sides for 3 minutes.

Place aioli on platter or 4 individual plates. Lay broccoli on aioli.

Sprinkle with pistachios.

Makes 4 servings.

Courtesy of Chef Charleen Badman of FnB Restaurant (p. 105)

Grilled Corn on the Cob

Chef Patrick Boll is another longtime Valley of the Sun chef, who sharpened his skills working with local celebrity chefs like Robert McGrath at places like Windows on the Green and Roaring Fork. Spotted Donkey Cantina isn't billed as an authentic Mexican restaurant. Instead, it's all about Southwestern-inspired dishes that are affordably priced and served in a festive setting. But the food is good and worth the visit, particularly this simple grilled corn on the cob recipe. It's perfect as a side dish for summertime barbecues or as a star-of-the-show appetizer.

Corn

Ear of corn in husk

Olive oil

Chipotle Mayonnaise (see recipe below)

Ground Cotija cheese

Chimayo chile powder

Grill corn in the husk until cooked through.

Remove from husk and brush with olive oil.

Place the corn back on the grill for a short time, turning to obtain the appropriate grill marks.

Brush the corn ears with Chipotle Mayonnaise (below).

Roll in ground Cotija cheese.

Sprinkle with chimayo chile powder.

Makes 1 serving.

Chipotle Mayonnaise

1 chipotle chile, diced
1 clove fresh garlic, chopped
Pinch of cilantro, chopped

Pinch of salt
¼ cup of your favorite
  mayonnaise

Combine mayonnaise, chile, garlic, and cilantro in a bowl and mix well.

Season with salt to taste.

Courtesy of Cliff Skoglund, owner, and Chef Patrick Boll of Spotted Donkey Cantina (p. 157)

Creamy Grits n' Sausage

Remember those years before 2008 when restaurant dining was all about over-the-top, glamorous fare? You know, the days when people didn't question the price on a $30 sandwich and ate it because it was trendy and "cool"? Yeah, those days pre-recession. I'm not one to mourn the past, though, especially given the drift toward neighborhood restaurants with more affordable, still delicious and innovative, food—like Beckett's Table. Chef Justin Beckett was one of several Greater Phoenix and Scottsdale chefs to make the switch with his Phoenix restaurant that's more about quality comfort food than flash. The following recipe epitomizes Beckett's new mindset. These creamy grits and sausage are a Beckett-made favorite of Howard Seftel, local food critic for the Arizona Republic.

Creamy Grits

1 quart chicken stock	**¼ block cream cheese**
1 cup yellow polenta	**Salt and white pepper to taste**
2 tablespoons butter	

Bring stock to a simmer in a heavy-bottomed pot.

Add polenta to the liquid and stir with a whisk, cooking on low heat for 20 to 25 minutes and stirring every couple of minutes. Be careful not to let the bottom stick and burn.

Remove from heat and add in the butter and cream cheese; stir until fully dissolved.

Season with salt and white pepper to taste.

Set aside while cooking the sausage mixture.

Sausage Mix

2 links Schreiner's Southwest turkey sausage (or any spicy turkey sausage)

2 links Schreiner's Andouille sausage

2 links Schreiner's Sweet Italian sausage

½ cup chopped oven-dried tomatoes

½ cup chopped onions

2 tablespoons whole grain mustard

1 teaspoon chopped garlic

¼ cup white wine

3 small pats of butter

Cook all sausages in 350-degree oven until cooked through, about 15 minutes.

Let cool and slice on a bias to create ½-inch ovals.

In a hot sauté pan, add all ingredients except the white wine and butter.

Sauté until caramelization starts to occur.

Deglaze with the white wine and add pats of butter to emulsify.

In a bowl, place two large spoonfuls of creamy grits in the center and spoon the sausage mixture on top of the grits. Pour some of the liquid over as well.

Garnish with your favorite herbs.

Makes 4 servings.

Courtesy of Chef Justin Beckett of Beckett's Table (p. 38)

Lamb Drumstick with Ginger Beer BBQ Sauce

Bryan's Black Mountain Barbecue in the North Valley is the real 'cue deal: Owner Bryan Dooley smokes meat over pecan wood chips, which he prefers over hickory because of their more subdued flavor. Meats—half-chicken, pulled chicken, St. Louis–style spare ribs, pulled pork, and beef brisket—are made with a Memphis-style rub and none are heavily sauced. Instead, the vinegar-based sauces take notes from Southern barbecue. Here, Dooley gives us the notes on his popular Ginger Beer BBQ Sauce, which pairs perfectly with the juicy, tender lamb shanks.

Ginger Beer BBQ Sauce

3 12-ounce beers	1 teaspoon lemon juice
2 ½ cups sugar	⅛ teaspoon cardamom
4 cups barbecue sauce	⅛ teaspoon allspice
1 ounce fresh ginger, julienned	2 bay leaves

Combine beer and sugar; simmer until reduced by half.

Add remaining ingredients and continue to simmer until sauce thickens.

Remove bay leaves and keep sauce warm.

Lamb Shanks

4 lamb shanks
                                    2 ounces of your preferred spice rub

Season lamb with spice rub and grill indirectly until tender, approximately 1½ hours. Or, place in smoker for approximately 5 hours.

When the shanks are tender, remove from heat and slather on the Ginger Beer BBQ Sauce.

Makes 4 servings.

Courtesy of Bryan Dooley, chef and owner of Bryan's Black Mountain Barbecue (p. 151)

Pollo Asado

Chef Doug Robson's name might scream "gringo!" but don't let it fool you. This guy was born and raised south of the border, which means his recipes didn't come out of some book; they come from life experience. And what could be better than that? Pollo Asado is one of the most classic and common Spanish recipes, and it is usually served for lunch. At Gallo Blanco Cafe, this recipe is served with a hearty helping of veggies but I find it pairs especially well with roasted potatoes. Add a simple green salad to the side and you've got one fantastic meal.

2 whole chickens

Marinade

2 limes, juiced
½ cup freshly squeezed orange juice, skins washed and saved
4 tablespoons minced garlic
2 teaspoons freshly ground pepper

½ cup cilantro
½ cup basil leaves, torn into small pieces
2 teaspoons paprika
¼ cup organic soy sauce

Glaze

1 cup honey

¼ cup quince paste

Wash chickens and pat dry.

Remove the wishbone surrounding the inside opening of neck cavity: Scrape the bone on both sides with a sharp knife, reach in and grab it with your fingers, and pull it out.

Use a sharp set of poultry shears, or a sharp knife, to carefully cut out the backbone, which will divide the chicken in half.

Use shears or a knife to trim away any protruding rib bones after the backbone is out.

Repeat with second chicken.

Prepare marinade by mixing lime juice, orange juice, garlic, pepper, cilantro, basil, paprika, and soy sauce in a large mixing bowl. Add washed orange skins.

Place chicken halves in a large, glass baking pan, skin side down.

Pour marinade over chickens.

Cover and refrigerate, turning occasionally, for about 2 to 4 hours.

Prepare a medium fire on the grill.

Place chicken on indirect heat, meat side facing up.

Cook it on this side for about 10 to 15 minutes.

Flip the chicken and grill another 10 to 15 minutes.

Baste skin with glaze and grill for another 5 to 10 minutes, flipping halfway through.

Check the internal temperature of the chicken, and when the thermometer reads 165 degrees, remove from grill.

Makes 4 servings.

Courtesy of Doug Robson, chef at Gallo Blanco Cafe & Bar (p. 76)

Chicken Pasta in a Parmesan Thyme Sauce

In addition to being another notch on Gilbert restaurateur Joe Johnston's belt, Liberty Market also is partly owned by David and Kiersten Traina. Chef David Traina began his career working for James Beard Award winner Roxsand Scocos at Paniolo Grill after striking a deal to work free for one month in order to learn from one of the Phoenix area's best chefs. Roxsand hired him after one month and, you'll be happy to know, renegotiated his pay to keep him on board full-time. Now, Traina delivers just as much passion and enthusiasm with his dishes at Liberty Market. The Chicken Pasta in a Parmesan Thyme Sauce is a local favorite.

¼ cup plus 2 tablespoons olive oil, divided

4 chicken breasts, sliced

1 pound cavatappi pasta (or another pasta of your choice)

2 zucchini, diced

2 yellow squash, diced

2 red bell peppers, diced

1 pound mushrooms, diced

Parmesan Thyme Sauce (see recipe below)

½ cup smoked mozzarella cheese, shredded

½ cup grated Parmesan cheese

Heat ¼ cup olive oil in pan and sauté chicken until cooked through.

Heat remaining olive oil in pan and sauté zucchini, squash, peppers, and mushrooms.

Cook pasta per directions on box.

After draining pasta, add Parmesan Thyme Sauce (you may choose not to use all of the sauce), chicken, vegetables, and smoked mozzarella. Stir until cheese is melted. Add salt and pepper to taste.

Divide pasta into 4 bowls and top with grated Parmesan cheese.

Parmesan Thyme Sauce

1 tablespoon olive oil	4 cups heavy cream
2 tablespoons minced shallot	1 cup grated Parmesan cheese
1½ teaspoon minced garlic	Salt and pepper to taste
1 tablespoon fresh thyme	

In a saucepan, heat oil and add shallots and garlic.

Sauté on low temperature until mixture is translucent and fragrant.

Add thyme and sauté for 2 minutes.

Add heavy cream and turn heat up to medium.

Stir in Parmesan and cook for 30 minutes, stirring frequently so as not to burn sauce. Add salt and pepper to taste.

Makes 4 servings.

Courtesy of Kiersten Traina, co-owner of Liberty Market (p. 194)

Oven-Steamed Sea Bass with Wild Mushrooms

Born and raised in Tokyo, Chef Nobuo Fukuda has been an Arizona chef for 30 years, starting as a green 20-year-old at the Benihana chain and evolving into one of the area's most celebrated culinary masters. Foodies love Fukuda because he honors Japanese traditions at the same time as he breaks them, blending the best of Eastern and Western cultures into one dining experience. In 2002, he opened the much-missed Sea Saw in downtown Scottsdale, a Japanese tapas bar that eventually earned him a James Beard Award in 2007.

From there, his star grew; Fukuda was named a "Chef to Watch" by John Mariani of Esquire *and received a handful of nods from top national publications, including* Food & Wine. *When Sea Saw closed, the entire community mourned. Luckily, Fukuda opened Nobuo at Teeter House in downtown Phoenix following the same principles of wildly inventive Japanese cuisine. His sea bass is one of the easier dishes for an at-home chef, but still wonderfully delicious.*

6 tablespoons unsalted butter, softened

2 garlic cloves, minced

½ pound shiitake mushrooms, stems discarded and caps thinly sliced

½ pound oyster mushrooms, thickly sliced

1 package enoki mushrooms

Salt and freshly ground pepper to taste

4 6-ounce sea bass fillets with skin, pin bones removed

2 tablespoons soy sauce

2 tablespoons sake

Preheat the oven to 500 degrees. In a small bowl, combine the butter and garlic. In a large skillet, melt half of the garlic butter.

Add the shiitake, oyster, and enoki mushrooms and cook over high heat, stirring occasionally, until tender and just beginning to brown, about 8 minutes. Season lightly with salt and pepper.

Tear off 4 sheets of heavy-duty aluminum foil, about 14 square inches, or parchment paper.

Spoon the mushrooms onto the foil squares and top with the fish fillets, skin side down.

Spread the remaining garlic butter over the fillets and drizzle with the soy sauce and sake.

Fold the foil or parchment over the fish and seal the edges of the packets. Set them seam-side-up on a sturdy baking sheet. Bake for 15 minutes, until the fish is tender.

Transfer the fish to plates, spoon the mushrooms and juices on top, and serve with rice and vegetables.

Makes 6 servings.

Courtesy of Chef Nobuo Fukuda of Nobuo at Teeter House (p. 79)

Burrata with Caponata

Taggia's Chef de Cuisine, James Siao, is inventive in his approach and use of local Arizona ingredients in the restaurant's coastal Italian cuisine. A member of the Slow Food movement, Siao supports local organic farmers and grows his own herbs in Taggia's patio garden. Caponata is a Sicilian eggplant dish, a cooked vegetable salad made from chopped fried eggplant and celery seasoned with sweetened vinegar and capers in a sweet and sour sauce. Numerous local variations of the ingredients exist with some versions adding olives, carrots, and green bell peppers, and others adding potatoes or pine nuts. Chef Siao combines his with burrata, an Italian cheese made from mozzarella and cream. Its name actually means "buttered" in Italian—no wonder!

Caponata

5 tablespoons olive oil

1½ pounds eggplant, unpeeled and cut into ½-inch cubes

1 medium red onion, diced

1 medium red pepper, diced

4 large garlic cloves, chopped

4 tablespoons red wine vinegar

4 tablespoons sugar

2 cups basic tomato sauce

2 tablespoons drained capers

⅓ cup chopped fresh basil

2 tablespoons raisins

Toasted pine nuts

Heat oil in a heavy large pot over medium heat.

Add eggplant, onion, red pepper, and garlic cloves. Sauté until eggplant is soft and brown, about 15 minutes.

Add red wine vinegar and sugar. Cover and simmer until eggplant and onion are very tender, stirring occasionally, for about 3 minutes. Then add tomato sauce and capers.

Season Caponata to taste with salt and pepper, continuing to stir. Simmer for 5 minutes.

Mix in fresh basil, raisins, and pine nuts. Transfer Caponata to serving bowl.

Serve warm, at room temperature, or cold.

Caponata can be made 2 days ahead; just cover and chill.

Serve burrata with a side of chilled Caponata, and sliced and grilled Ciabatta bread.

Makes 2 servings.

Courtesy of James Siao, chef at Taggia (p. 125)

Sticky Toffee Pudding

When rumors first started to fly about Chef Aaron Chamberlin opening St. Francis, local foodies waited on pins and needles, practically salivating at just the thought of it. Why? Well, eat at St. Francis one time and you'll understand. But Chamberlin's reputation preceded him, that's for sure. His résumé is packed solid with big names like Michel Richard and Jean-Georges Vongerichten. When he finally graced Phoenix with his presence, he worked at popular local spots like La Grande Orange and Chelsea's Kitchen. The first time I dug into a helping of Chamberlin's sticky toffee pudding, I wanted to dance. I wanted to sing. I wanted to run out the door with three more servings of the stuff. But, instead, I decided to snag the recipe and share it with you.

Cakes

¾ cup dates, pitted and slivered
1¼ cup warm water
1 teaspoon baking soda
1 cup + 1 tablespoon flour
1 teaspoon baking powder

½ teaspoon salt
¾ cup brown sugar
1 large egg
1 teaspoon vanilla
¼ cup unsalted butter, melted

Preheat oven to 350 degrees.

Combine half of the dates with water and baking soda. Soak 5 minutes.

Whisk flour, baking powder, and salt together.

Process remaining dates with brown sugar in a food processor until you get a coarse, sandy texture.

Drain soaked dates, set aside, and add liquid to food processor with egg, vanilla, and melted butter. Process until smooth.

Fold date mixture into flour mixture. Fold in soaked dates.

Spray and flour 4 ramekins. Fill ramekins with batter about two-thirds full.

Put in hotel pan. Fill a quarter of the way up with boiling water, cover tightly with foil, and bake approximately 40 minutes.

Poke a few holes in the finished product.

Toffee Sauce

½ cup butter
1 cup brown sugar
½ teaspoon salt

1 cup heavy cream, whipped
½ cup rum
½ lemon, squeezed for juice

Melt butter and whisk in brown sugar and salt.

Cook until sugar is dissolved and it turns slightly browner, 3 to 4 minutes.

Slowly add cream and rum, whisking constantly. Reduce and let simmer until frothy.

Remove from heat and add lemon juice.

Top cakes with warm Toffee Sauce and serve with a scoop of sweet cream gelato.

Courtesy of Chef Aaron Chamberlin of St. Francis (p. 50)

Appendices

Appendix A: Greater Phoenix & Scottsdale Eateries by Cuisine

Appendix B: Dishes, Specialties & Specialty Food

Index